The complete paintings of

Botticelli

Introduction by **Michael Levey**

Notes and catalogue by **Gabriele Mandel**

Harry N. Abrams, Inc. *Publishers* New York

Classics of the World's Great Art

Editor
Paolo Lecaldano

**International
Advisory Board**
Gian Alberto dell'Acqua
André Chastel
Douglas Cooper
Lorenz Eitner
Enrique Lafuente Ferrari
Bruno Molajoli
Carlo L. Ragghianti
Xavier de Salas
David Talbot Rice
Jacques Thuillier
Rudolf Wittkower

*This series of books is
published in Italy by Rizzoli
Editore, in France by
Flammarion, in the United
Kingdom by Weidenfeld and
Nicolson, in the United States
by Harry N. Abrams, Inc.,
in Spain by Editorial
Noguer and in Switzerland by
Kunstkreis*

Standard Book Number
8109–5501–6
Library of Congress Catalogue
Card Number 75-85175
© Copyright in Italy by
Rizzoli Editore, 1967
Printed and bound in Italy

Table of contents

Introduction

We must always be grateful to the nineteenth century for rediscovering Botticelli; yet to some extent he is in need of being discovered again.

The sudden rush of fame after three centuries of real neglect propelled an image now seen to be only too patently of nineteenth-century devising. Although it has long been clear that Botticelli was not a willful creator of sickly *fin de siècle* Virgins, it has by no means been established what sort of artist he was. And then the sheer familiarity of pictures like the *Primavera* and the *Birth of Venus* has induced a sort of weariness of the eye, only enhanced by a general, welcome tendency to place the Florentine early Renaissance in proper perspective, no longer the awesome isolated peak of Western art which it once was. Nor would it be surprising if at least English writers hesitated to add more words to the often beautiful if perverse appreciations of Botticelli evoked in nineteenth-century England.

It may even be asked if Botticelli is a Renaissance figure at all, but it is as well not to formulate a concept of "the Renaissance" as though it had been an art movement comparable to Impressionism or *Die Brücke*. Botticelli is not known to have executed sculpture, designed buildings, written poems or theoretical treatises. He quite fails to be the *uomo universale* of popular Renaissance myth, yet it would be rash to disqualify him from being of the Renaissance for defects which happen also to be Titian's. As long as any viable concept exists of "Renaissance", it is likely that Titian will be admitted within it. Like him, Botticelli was primarily a painter. Apart from the special case of his Dante illustrations, drawings by him are remarkably few. As a painter – as a highly intelligent if not intellectual artist who created a highly personal and sophisticated style of expression – Botticelli should be recognized as indeed part of the Renaissance. So far from being, as is sometimes supposed, retardataire, he was if anything in advance of his period – having more in common with Pontormo than with his contemporary Ghirlandaio.

His paintings – all of them illustrated in one form or another in this book – are distinguished by a revolutionary, innovatory refinement, using the word in its original technical sense of purifying and separating a substance from extraneous matter. Any idea of Botticelli as decorating or ornamenting surfaces, adding to things, is quite wrong. It is the first way in which he differs from his master, Fra Filippo Lippi, whose work was aptly described by a fifteenth-century Florentine as "grazioso et ornato et artificioso sopra modo". It is incidentally worth noting that what another percipient contemporary thought remarkable about Botticelli's pictures was their "aria virile" – a sharp contradiction to any lingering associations of languor.

Botticelli's refinement is a stripping away of inessentials and of merely distracting surface naturalism, but it is not a rejection of nature. In this process he can reasonably be paralleled with Klee. Perhaps it is no more than chance that both are masters of marvelous line; what is less uncertain is that both painters had studied nature intensely, and what they produce are concentrated, economical images more vital and essential than any transcript of ordinary nature as we see it. As rigorously as Leonardo must Botticelli have observed the natural form of a shell – itself in hard thinness, fluted curves and faintest translucence, a perfect symbol of his style. Botticelli studied it, however, only to transform it into magically giant form and make it the floating vehicle supporting Venus across the waves to the seashore of Cythera (Pls. XLIV–V). That island is shown with a jagged coastline extending from foreground to horizon, without aerial perspective and with scarcely any three-dimensional modelling. One long memorable line indents the pale promontories, so many green spearpoints fronting a liquid element that does not resemble the sea but in which one perceives what Klee called "the process of flowing". The shore with its few trees is the barest scaffolding of nature: three gilt-flecked poles are stuck in velvet-soft green mould and become a myrtle grove.

Yet we "read" this picture with no more difficulty than we do the much more naturalistically imitative *Baptism of Christ* (in the Uffizi) by Verrocchio and Leonardo, a famous picture which makes a fascinating comparison – in subject and composition as well as style – and which almost certainly precedes Botticelli's *Birth of Venus*. It is the Verrocchio-Leonardo naturalism which seems doomed, timid and even inartistic, in pursuit of something that would ultimately be satisfied by photography. Anyway, it is a confusion of thought to believe that Christ's baptism will necessarily take on greater reality if it is depicted in what seems illusionistically like a real river in a real, modeled landscape. The way is opened toward Holman Hunt's *Light of the World*.

Behind Botticelli's picture is intense conviction and intense confidence about the power of art. Not merely is there pleasure for us in enjoying the world he has built up – not copied – out of nature, but the conviction and confidence give significant reality to what is depicted. There is therefore, paradoxically or not, a religious credibility about his pagan goddess which marks a new attitude to mythological subject-matter. Artistically, she certainly challenges the Christian god. It would be absurd to deduce from that anything about Botticelli's own personal religious belief; and the nineteenth century notoriously detected in him ambiguities that really lay in its own perplexed attitude to Christianity. Yet, the artistic conviction of Botticelli's picture is reinforced by the likelihood that it has ethical and moral significance; it was probably painted not just as a large-scale decorative canvas but as a didactic one. A beautiful ruling deity remains its theme and the centre of its composition. That too could be sensed, long before modern scholarship indicated neo-Platonic philosophy behind the picture; and we should honor Pater for treating it so seriously and recognizing in its Venus "the depository of a great power over men".

The process of stripping away appearances which is an actual physical result – accounting for the disconcerting effect of Botticelli's work and its neglect during periods of robust naturalism – is something pursued not merely then to give clean-cut, artistically beautiful images in themselves, but to affect the spectator emotionally. To Botticelli's keenness of line must be added his psychological keenness. He had studied the nature of leaves and shells (a fine conch appearing in *Mars and Venus*, Pls. XXXVI–VII), but penetration of human nature is the most remarkable of his studies.

It led him to the very opposite of sculptural effects in painting, though that does not mean he had not looked at, particularly, Donatello's sculpture. The anatomical emphasis of Castagno and Antonio Pollaiuolo – both men older than he – also affected him, but he rapidly recognized that in art states of emotion must dictate beyond muscular behavior in ordinary life. His figures mime their states of mind. In extremes of grief and joy, they are like reeds shaken in the wind. Bending without breaking, the troubled Virgin receives the angel's salutation (Pl. L). Around the Virgin and Child in the *Madonna of the Pomegranate* (Pl. XXXVIII) six angel heads express adoration in a tour-de-force of varied poses and significance, none of them repeating the other. In the tall *Pietà* (Pl. LVIII), the very shape of which helps to tauten emotion, grief grows so intense that one Mary has become a faceless bundle of draperies, held together by two quivering hands. And, most marvelously of all, in the *Mystic Nativity* (Pl. LXII) heaven's joy at the event is expressed by that dance of interlinked angels in a sky of gold and luminous blue: twelve figures borne up less by their wings than by utter ecstasy, an ecstasy communicated to the curling folds of their dresses and even to their scrolls uncoiling like suddenly released springs.

What is conveyed is not always a violent extreme of emotion. In the *Mystic Nativity* the foreground pairs of angels embracing mortals are wonderful certainly, but well known; less familiar is the detail (Pl. LXIII) where an angel bends over a still bewildered shepherd, one hand tenderly reassuring at his shoulder, the other stretched out indicating the newly born Child with such urgency that the arm seems almost detached, so unrealistically long and thin has it become. Yet, within the arrow-like wedge formed between the angel's two arms, Botticelli finds space for the shepherd slowly to push back his hood, paying homage as the significance of the scene gradually becomes apparent to him. These poignantly vivid images compress all – and indeed more than – words can say about heaven and earth, about inspiration and mere human understanding, and they also crystallize that faith in divinely peaceful order coming to the world which Botticelli records more cryptically in the Greek inscription at the top of the picture.

The *Mystic Nativity* may well be one of the last of Botticelli's surviving paintings, but it should not be treated as some abrupt palinode, either artistically or personally. Far from representing any break with his early style, it is a culmination of many tendencies. Along with formal motifs, touches of nature observed are still apparent and here he unexpectedly introduces flecks of pinkish early morning cloud which rim round the archaic gold of heaven. Since Botticelli had always been a painter of religious pictures, and had constantly evolved fresh versions of the Nativity theme (see Pls. IV–V, VII, XIII, and XXVIII–IX), there is no need to postulate a dramatic conversion due to Savonarola, old age or the troubles of Italy. That the *Mystic Nativity* is passionate does not mean that its creator was neurotic – a dangerous term to apply to someone so long dead, about whose personality so little is known, but a term still being used of Botticelli in a current popular dictionary of art and artists.

To understand Botticelli we must concentrate on his art, not bothering about preconceptions of naturalism or what we would have supposed of a painter living in late fifteenth-century Florence. As well as ways in which he may be contrasted with, for example, Leonardo, there are others in which he can be seen to be remarkably similar. Even their usual stylistic differences disappear in the fragments of Botticelli's late *Adoration of the Magi* (here no. 154 A, B, C). Both artists gave new significance to old-established subject-matter by making it psychologically convincing; and in their work the figures are wrought into being themselves works of art.

Botticelli's standard remains always that of the imagination; its truths are what his art ultimately enshrines, rather than those of science or the natural physical world. Nothing, perhaps, better illustrates the unique mixture he achieved than his portraits, convincing as individual likenesses, though of one family in sheer, deliberate beauty beyond any possibility in nature, disdaining suggestions of surface texture and yet vibrant with vitality. The result becomes the truth – and hence the conviction of which his paintings are full. We may well feel tempted to make him say, with Keats, "I never can feel certain of any truth but from a clear perception of its Beauty." And with those words Keats began some comments on Italian Renaissance painting.

MICHAEL LEVEY

An outline of the artist's critical history

Botticelli was much admired during his lifetime. Suffice it to mention, in addition to all the work he did for the Medicis, his public commissions and his summons to Rome to work in the Sistine Chapel. But his fame was not enduring. Even Vasari (not to mention Leonardo's rebuke) tends to undervalue Botticelli's memory through anecdotal pleasantries (which he reserved for artists he did not much admire) and praise that was modified by serious reservations. Vasari seems to have considered him an artist who wasted his talents in the pursuit of insufficiently high ideals. The experts charged by the Grand Duke of Tuscany in 1598 to list works worth preserving do not mention Botticelli's paintings. And aside from the paraphrasing of Vasari by a Baldinucci or an Orlandi, there was no mention of Botticelli in the next two centuries. By the end of the eighteenth century Botticelli was practically unknown. Even Lanzi only recalls the Sistine frescoes and "many paintings with small figures," which – this usually alert scholar suprisingly asserts – might be mistaken for works by Mantegna if the faces were more "beautiful." Botticelli's fate was no better during the Neoclassical period. It was only in the late Romantic period that Ruskin became interested in Botticelli's style and summed up the artist's expressive qualities as "a play of pure line." The attention of Ruskin and his Pre-Raphaelite friends was also attracted to the moral subjects of Botticelli's work, with equal fervor but less success in the outcome. So that, after the penetrating discovery of the inner turmoil that even showed through the artist's cerebral finesse, there soon emerged – fostered by some of the Decadent writers, such as Péladan (*Le vice suprême*, 1884) and Mirbeau ("Orphelins," in *Buveurs d'âmes*, 1889) – the untenable image of a day-dreaming, sighing, neurotic and morbid "primitive." This aroused the Positivists, who were alarmed by an alleged lack of virility [Müntz] in Botticelli, and the more academic critics mistook Botticelli's highly refined stylization for weak draftsmanship, unskilled handling of perspective and slight color sense. (See, for a late example, Mesnil [1938].) How much the interpretation of the Decadents misled some criticism, binding it to external aspects of Botticelli's work, is amply demonstrated even in such recent criticism as that of A. Venturi. At the same time the great popularity of Botticelli was finally assured.

It was Berenson – despite the impediment of Pater's "pained frustration" – who rediscovered the high poetry of the vibration of line and the musical coherence of Botticelli. Yashiro, L. Venturi and, even more, Bettini and Argan have carried on this analysis. At the same time, other scholars – Ulmann, Bode, Gamba, Mesnil and Salvini – have set about a careful examination of the surviving corpus.

Sandro di Botticello, a [very] excellent painter in panel and wall: his things have a virile air with fine sense and careful proportion. Philippino di frate Philippi [Filippino Lippi], a fine disciple of the above-mentioned and son of the most singular master of his times: his things have a sweeter air, [but] I do not think they have as much art . . . *Letter to Ludovico il Moro from an agent in Florence, c. 1485*

. . . [the Bellinis, Botticelli, Filippino Lippi, Ghirlandaio, Perugino, Mantegna and Melozzo da Forlì] always with plummet and compass proportioning their works conduct them to an admirable perfection. In such manner that they appear not human but divine to our eyes. And in all their figures it seems that only the soul is missing. L. PACIOLI, *Summa de arithmetica, geometria, proportioni et proportionalità*, 1498

. . . Alexandro Botechiella has been much recommended to me as an excellent painter . . . F. DE' MALATESTI, *Letter to Isabella d'Este*, 1502

. . . Likewise rapid in work and famous in painting were the brothers Ghirlandaio. Nor is our Sandro considered inferior to Zeuxis, even though he fooled the birds with his painting of grapes. Nor is less praise made of the brothers Pollaiuolo . . . U. VERINI, *De illustratione urbis Florentiae*, 1503

He can never be universal who does not love equally all things in painting; so that if one did not care for the landscape, he would consider it a thing of short and simple study, as our Botticella said, that such study was vain, because if one threw a sponge full of various colors against a wall, it would leave a spot in which one could see a beautiful landscape. LEONARDO DA VINCI, *Trattato della pittura*, c. 1505

Sandro then deserved great praise for all the pictures he made, in which he put diligence and loving work; . . . G. VASARI, *Le Vite*, 1568

. . . he had such an extravagant and unquiet mind that he found stability in nothing . . . a very good painter. F. BALDINUCCI, *Notizie de' professori del disegno*, 1681

An extravagant and bizarre mind that acquired all the necessary documents for painting in Filippo Lippi and thus appeared to be a great master. P. A. ORLANDI, *Abecedario pittorico*, 3rd ed., 1753

Sandro drew with such mastery and taste . . . He was likewise vivid and beautiful in coloring, adorning his historical pictures with many and well-arranged figures, and showing in that way that he was not inferior in invention to others of his time. The technique of mordanting gold highlighting of figures was still practiced in that age, and Sandro, among others, succeeded with much assurance, never failing to do so whatever the color of the figures' dress. He had much grace in arranging the small figures, which he drew with much care. M. LASTRI, *L'Etruria pittrice*, 1791

. . . famous in that time and still known in picture collections for many paintings with small figures, in which he might sometimes be mistaken for Mantegna if he were more beautiful with the heads. Some panels still survive, but nothing to compare with what he did in the Sistine. There one can barely recognize the Sandro of Florence. The Temptation of Christ adorned with a very large Temple with a large number of offering-bearers in the atrium; Moses aiding the daughters of Jethro against the Midianite shepherds with such a beautiful display of brightly colored raiment; others he did are executed with such vitality and inventiveness that he seems to have far exceeded himself. The same can be seen in others: what can be done to their skill by the life of a city accustomed to enlarge ideas and the judgment of a public that is barely satisfied by the good because its eye is accustomed to the marvelous. L. LANZI, *Storia pittorica della Italia*, 1795–6

. . . I think one can say that Botticelli was inferior to Ghirlandaio in vitality and beauty of coloring, for [the former's] were dull and uniform, and in nobility and grandeur of raiment and composition, in which Sandro, with that supremely capricious genius of his . . . sometimes appeared strange and confused. F. RANALLI, *Storia delle belle arti in Italia*, 1845

I have said that the peculiar character of Botticelli is the result of a blending in him of a sympathy for humanity in its uncertain condition, its attractiveness, its investiture at rarer moments in a character of loveliness and energy, with his consciousness of the shadow upon it of the great things from which it shrinks, and that this conveys into his work somewhat more than painting usually attains of the true complexion of humanity.

He paints the story of the goddess of pleasure in other episodes besides that of her birth from the sea, but never without some shadow of death in the grey flesh and wan flowers. He paints Madonnas, but they shrink from the pressure of the divine child, and plead in unmistakable undertones for a warmer, lower, humanity. W. PATER, *Studies in the History of the Renaissance*, 1873

Botticelli was a man of such lively imagination that he was never unable to take on the most difficult problems of painting. His means, it is true, were not always at the level of his will, but his habitual daring soon gave him an exceptional position, which explains why he was so long considered superior to Domenico Ghirlandaio. In the Church of Ognissanti in Florence one can still see Botticelli's *St Augustine* facing the St Jerome that Ghirlandaio painted in 1480. It is Botticelli that triumphs, although he displays less nobility than his contemporary. J. A. CROWE, *Gazette des Beaux-Arts*, 1886

In fact, the mere subject, and even representation in general, was so indifferent to Botticelli, that he appears almost as if haunted by the idea of communicating the *unembodied* values of touch and movement. Now there is a way of rendering even tactile values with almost no body, and that is by translating them as faithfully as may be into values of movement. For instance: – we want to render the roundness of a wrist without the slightest touch of either light or shade; we simply give the movement of the wrist's outline and the movement of the drapery as it falls over it, and the roundness is communicated to us almost entirely in terms of movement. . . . Take . . . the lines that render the movements of the tossing hair, the fluttering draperies, and the dancing waves in *The Birth of Venus* – take these lines alone with all their power of stimulating our imagination of movement, and what do we have? Pure values of movement abstracted, unconnected with any representation whatever. This kind of line, then, being the quintessence of movement, has, like the essential elements in all the arts, a power of stimulating our imagination and of directly communicating life. Well! imagine an art made up entirely of these quintessences of movement-values, and you will have something that holds the same relation to representation that music holds to speech – and this art exists, and is called linear decoration. In this art of arts Sandro Botticelli may have had rivals in Japan and elsewhere in the East, but in Europe never. To its demands he was ready to sacrifice everything that habits acquired under Filippo and Pollaiuolo – and his employers! – would permit. The representative element was for him a mere libretto. . . . B. BERENSON, *The Italian Painters of the Renaissance*, 1896

Botticelli was a disciple of Fra Filippo, but this can be seen only in his very first works. They were two completely different temperaments; the friar with his open smile and his continual good-natured complacency with the things of this world; Botticelli, instead, tormented, ardent, always inwardly excited, an artist to whom the pictorial surface had very little to say, who expresses himself in violent lines and always succeeds in giving his faces fullness of character and expression. . . . He takes religious history seriously and, with the years, this seriousness increases, making him abandon all complacency in external form. His beauty has something melting in it, and even when he smiles it is only a fleeting flash. How little joy there is in the dance of the Graces in *Primavera*, and what sort of bodies are these! . . . Elegance bursts forth in the depiction of grass and flowers on the ground, and of the transparent fabrics, and almost reaches the fantastic. But it was not in Botticelli's temperament to stop and contemplate a detail. Even in the nude he soon tires of the too precise detail and tries to achieve a simpler representation through broader strokes. That he was an extraordinary drafts-man is even granted by Vasari, despite his Michelangelesque training: his line is always alive and full of character, it has something hasty about it. In representing a rapid movement it is incomparably effective: he even manages to give movement to large masses, and when he organizes the picture totally around a central point, something specifically new is born, something of decisive importance for the future. H. WÖLFFLIN, *Die klassische Kunst*, 1899

This intimate taste for lower feelings which is Botticelli's charm is in itself a sign of weakness, a lack of universality. Botticelli's work is lively, but the life it embodies is not high and desirable. One can say of him what one can say of any man: one can take him or leave him. It might be better to leave him. His lack of universality leads him to exaggeration, a lack of measure. If one has too much to do with him, one loses the true sense of life. His return to popularity coincides with the separation of the world of art from that of everyday activity. His taste for weakness is not an attribute of the ordinary man nor of the superior man. It is a refuge, to which it is nice to withdraw for a while far from the world, but it is not a place to live. It follows, then, that the pre-dominance of Botticelli, or of an art like his, means that, for most people, art is outside life and different from it. And this would be the death of art.

That is why, in judging Botticelli, it is better not to stop for the capricious charm of his Madonnas and Venuses, his nervousness, his impassioned outbursts, his half-tones, his faulty drawing, but rather notice his sustained color, the vigorous arrangement of certain groups, certain forms, and the calm and dignified force of his conception of man. The union of strength and weakness, complexity and simplicity, energy and indecision make Botticelli a personality that can charm and seduce us. But his strength alone allows us to enjoy his weakness and, what is more important still, this strength can be, and has been, a guide for others to create the finest works. A. P. OPPÉ, *Botticelli*, 1913

Supporters of modern movements in Art are crying so much against the imitation of Nature, that there are many cultured people who tend not to approve of a well-finished piece of realistic work, because of its faithful representation of Nature. In the case of Botticelli, appreciative critics began to make much of him as an artist of "presentation" instead of "representation," by which I mean, as an artist of line-function, not dependent upon the representation of Nature. That, I agree, is essentially true of Botticelli, as we shall see. But in their enthusiasm in having discovered the merit of "presentation" almost for the first time in European Art, critics were carried away so far as to imagine that the appreciation of "presentation" could only be at the expense of the merit of "representation." These two are logically, and only logically, incongruous. In human experience they can go side by side, and in plastic art both of them must exercise their

psychic influences. More than that: in plastic art it is the "repre-sentation" of visual Nature which is indispensable, the require-ment of which differentiates it from other arts, as music and decorative design. The "presentation" element is directly life-giving, and constitutes a powerful psychological function in Art, but it depends upon realistic formation for arriving at full plastic expression. Botticelli's art was a rare gift in Europe, in the fact that, amidst the too exclusive cult of Realism, he almost alone was capable of "presentation" in Art, free and ethereal; all the more do I bless fortune that he was born in an age ardently occupied with what he by nature lacked, which was indispens-able in making him a great plastic painter. Y. YASHIRO, *Botticelli*, 1925

. . . velvet flowers are his women with their arching lineaments, long pallid eyes, and languid heads weighted down with masses of gold; swarms of butterflies the lined lights of the sea, the tiny leaves that envelope, but barely touch the bushes that still shiver with winter frost . . . the exotic charm of the irregular faces, the febrile and languid rhythm of the bodies arouse impressions of music in the soul of the observer. Contributing to the charm of Botticelli's visions are the muted tones which he favored, not-withstanding his love of velvets and sparkling gold: pale skies, colorless and limpid, water of a tenuous green, roses without splendor, with a faded pink glaze, or brown velvet, olive flesh tones . . . or grays mixed with silver . . . tints subdued in pallor, which accompany with a melancholy note, subdued and grave, the varied rhythm of the composition. A. VENTURI, *Botticelli*, 1925

What makes Botticelli unique in his time and raises him above so many artists that were formally more perfect is not only this poetic fantasy, which Piero di Cosimo only a short time later shared to no less a degree, albeit in less beautiful forms; but that sense of proportion between figures and space, linear rhythm that joins figures and groups in harmoniously arranged masses, an idealistic delicacy of color that harmonizes color and gold high-lighting. And above all that absorbed inner sensitivity, intense spiritual passion, that emanates from his creations . . . C. GAMBA, *Botticelli*, 1936

His preference for line as against chiaroscuro or color is a limit-ation of his genius, but within that limitation it is his strength, his glory. He is one of the greatest poets of line whom history records. Antonio Pollaiuolo taught him how much artistic profit may be extracted from the outline, when it is conceived incisively, both as regards the construction of the human body in its function of relief, and in order to suggest movement, as an accentuation or impulse. Botticelli dreams fantastic arabesques, slow and continuous dance-rhythms, the gracefulness of line; and he knows how to realize them in their function of relief and move-ment. Nothing can take from his line its contemplative value, its fairy-like delicacy, even when it is based on natural vision. And natural vision thus become the form of his dream. . . . The pre-sentation of the figure, or groups of figures, realized in line, assumes such importance in Botticelli's mind that he sacrifices to it the illustrative effectiveness of the story or allegory and the relationship between the various episodes. . . . But we must remember that if the ensemble existed, the magical effect of the individual figures would be less intense. They would no longer emerge from mystery like the figures of a dream. Yet it is possible to discover a rhythm in Botticelli's compositions: the *rhythm of detail*, which finds its justification in the very intensity with which each detail is conceived.   L. VENTURI, *Botticelli*, 1937

. . . He had an open, curious, inquiring spirit that went far beyond the problems he had to face in his artistic activity; his was a vital and subtle intelligence . . . if he was not altogether wanting in will power, coherence and inner discipline, they were weak or intermittent. Hence his hesitations, his waverings, his back-tracking. . . . [In *The Mystic Nativity*] Botticelli gets away from geometric composition in depth, in which figures are smaller the farther away they are: he has filled his canvas as if it were a page in a missal and arranges his figures on various planes. The Virgin dominates everyone by her size, and she is even larger than the foreground figures, who, in linear perspective, should be larger than she is. It is all a symbolic view. . . . All realism is absent from this composition, and the elongated and downcast forms are drawn with a certain negligence and *gaucherie* that must be intended, since we know what Botticelli could have done. The faces have no specific expression and feeling is shown chiefly in gesture, in the moving line.   J. MESNIL, *Botticelli*, 1938

Berenson noted that Botticelli preferred presentation to re-presentation: each element of the picture – be it a single figure or a group of figures – is seen as a "presence" so immediate that any interest in coordinated narration comes second. [L.] Venturi says that this interest in the detail creates the nuclei of Botticelli's composition: the intensity with which the detail is felt and rendered in line determines that "rhythm of detail" which is the secret of Botticelli's art. Venturi's ela-boration makes Berenson's idea critically more concrete; and it dispels the doubt, which still survived in Berenson's idea, that there is a certain instability in Botticelli's idiom. . . . And to remove the shadow of a doubt that this is determined by today's usual taste, it is worth noting what has now become a commonplace: that for Botticelli this isolation of figural units means properly focusing the image: the "presentation" of details is the result of the necessity of reinforcing the center of rhythm, the strengthening through an absorbing center com-position that, left horizontally, would result in a Lippi-like descriptiveness. . . . Thus Botticelli is not fragmentary, a creator of little mottoes deviating from the refined culture of his time: he really composes, even in the large Sistine frescoes; it is just that the unity of these compositions does not lie, classically, in the ordered balance of perspective planes but in the very rhythmic series, which here displays a careful exactitude of order in the lyrical coherence and an extraordinarily *legato* unity of stanza: an extremely tight pictorial texture, whose reverse, in a manner of speaking, would display a warp of continually returning rhythms. S. BETTINI, *Botticelli*, 1942

The painting of Botticelli . . . marks the crisis of the great systems of figural order that had been elaborated in the first half of the fifteenth century. It is the crisis of the concept of space and perspective; that of form in the sense of knowledge or representa-tion of nature; that of *historia* as the dramatic depiction of human actions; that of the moral and religious character of art; the

crisis, finally, of the social function of the artist as a representative of a higher craftsmanship, and that of the productive capacity of a community. Art too tends to the beautiful, as do philosophic thought and the study of the ancients and human action; or rather, art is the specific process of the search for the beautiful, so that the artist's work is rather an example than a genuine creation. . . . For the first time, a Renaissance painter tends to the "beautiful" as a supreme end. (I use the term "painter" advisedly, for there had already been an artist, Agostino di Duccio, who had, albeit less clearly, the same need.) It is undeniable that Botticelli, seeing in art the actualization or "practical moment" of an esthetic ideal, somehow went back to certain medieval elements of the late Gothic. But his idea of *pulchritudo* is no longer linked to the Thomistic theses of beauty and the harmony of Creation, in the sense of sensible manifestations of the perfection of the Creator. Thus one can say that Botticelli's painting, albeit deeply permeated by a religious aspiration, actually achieves only a vague "lay" religious character.   G. C. ARGAN, *Botticelli*, 1957

The clever costumer, the intrepid and inventive narrator that Botticelli was, followed the innovations of the Florentine gold-smiths and illuminators of 1460. He did not have to create his types, his turning silhouettes, his gauze apparel, his complicated hair-dos, his romantic attitudes and sentimental reversals. But he recreated this lively and gracious repertory; he had less work in enriching it than in purifying it. He knew how to make out-lines more precise, adjust folds, curve figures, interweave and loosen movements with the continuous effect of an arabesque. This small Romanesque world is almost recreated from within, recomposed, and carried back to a sharper sense of order, a deeper elegance, a more rigorous imitation – it is subjected to a subtler poetic. Sandro is a distiller, and his material is the narrative repertory, elegance accentuated by a Gothic sense of the precious, of the Florentine *ateliers*. The longilineal female type, unstable, with a short nose and a triangular chin, a distant gaze, in this light and delicate art seems almost to await the coming and the poetic gift of Botticelli.   A. CHASTEL, *Botticelli*, 1957

Thus the accent shifts in the various phases of the artist's long career, but his expression is unified in essence, and his poetic world coherent. Its coherence is mirrored in the consistent development of a style characterized by a line that asserts, more or less directly, the values of volume and space. Botticelli's inspiration culminates at the point where movement transcends pose, life becomes memory, reality becomes image and symbol, and history is fixed in the crystal of myth. R. SALVINI, "Botticelli," *Encyclopedia of World Art*, 1963

No great painter of the Quattrocento more than Botticelli took such pleasure in varying the schemes of "divine proportion." Some of them . . . display an undeniable scientific knowledge. But where did he get this knowledge? Let us recall that he was admitted at a very early age to the Medici court, where he met Humanists and poets – whose influence is reflected in his mytho-logical representations – and the more important philosophers and mathematicians. Who knows whether between these men and the young painter there was not established a close collaboration in the development of clearly geometric schemata . . .

Botticelli's geometry provides the necessary light to understand fully the meaning of the praise of him written in 1485–6 [*sic*] and preserved in the Milan archives: his works "have a virile air with fine sense and careful proportion." It should not be forgotten that, in that period, "proportion" indicated the equivalence of the two relationships that, geometrically joined, composed the regulatory schemata . . .

Among the lines, all articulated together to form a geometrical figure, Botticelli excelled in distinguishing those which could guide him in situating single figures or groups of figures; and these lines justified their positioning and their gestures, which expressed perfect serenity or ardor.   E. MAILLARD, *Botticelli*, 1965

The paintings in color

*In the captions to the color plates the actual
size (width) of the painting or detail
reproduced in each plate is indicated in
parentheses.*

ATE I   MADONNA AND CHILD WITH ANGELS   Naples, Gallerie Nazionali di Capodimonte
Whole (71 cm.)

FORTITUDE Florence, Uffizi
Whole (87 cm.)

PLATE III   PORTRAIT OF A MAN WITH A MEDAL OF COSIMO THE ELDER Florence, Uffizi
Detail (actual size)

PLATES IV-V   THE ADORATION OF THE MAGI London, National Gallery
Whole (141 cm.)

PLATE VI   THE ADORATION OF THE MAGI London, National Gallery
Detail (actual size)

PLATE VIII   THE ADORATION OF THE MAGI London, National Gallery
Detail (26 cm.)

PLATE IX   THE ADORATION OF THE MAGI London, National Gallery
Detail (26 cm.)

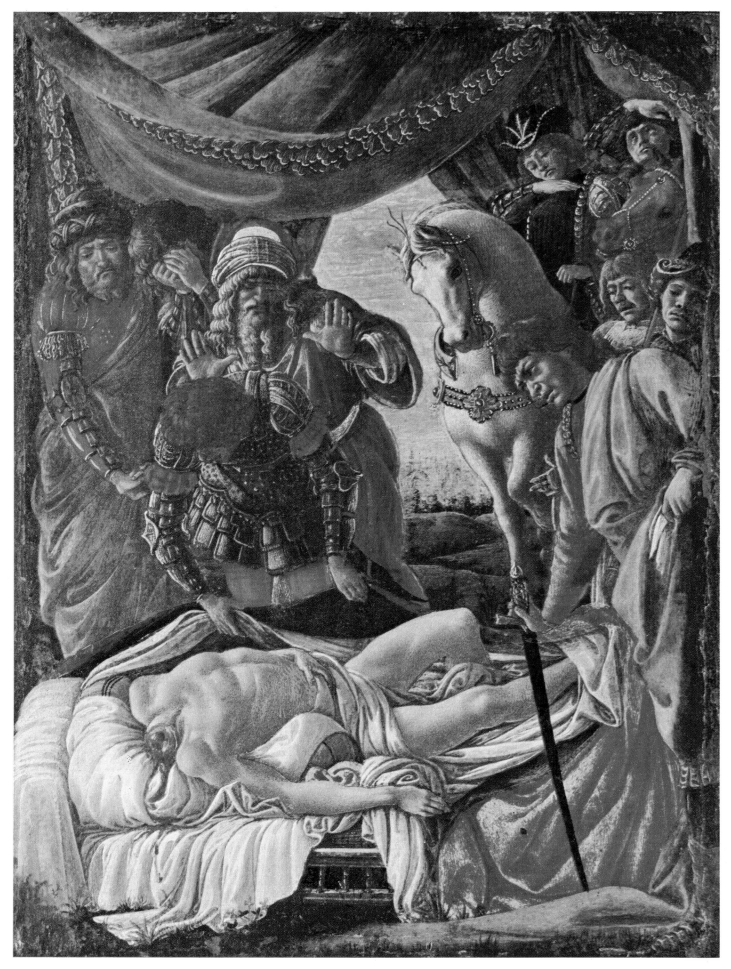

PLATE X   THE FINDING OF THE BODY OF HOLOFERNES Florence, Uffizi
Whole (25 cm.)

THE RETURN OF JUDITH Florence, Uffizi
Whole (24 cm.)

PLATE XII   PORTRAIT OF A YOUNG WOMAN Florence, Pitti
Whole (40 cm.)

PLATE XIV   THE ADORATION OF THE MAGI Florence, Uffizi
Detail (28 cm.)

PLATE XV   THE ADORATION OF THE MAGI Florence, Uffizi
Detail (10.5 cm.)

PLATES XVI-XVII   PRIMAVERA Florence, Uffizi
Whole (314 cm.)

PLATE XVIII   PRIMAVERA Florence, Uffizi
Detail (56 cm.)

ATE XIX   PRIMAVERA Florence, Uffizi
Detail (61 cm.)

PLATE XX   PRIMAVERA Florence, Uffizi
Detail (73 cm.)

PLATE XXI   PRIMAVERA Florence, Uffizi
Detail (29 cm.)

PLATE XXII   MADONNA OF THE BOOK   Milan, Museo Poldi Pezzoli
Whole (39.5 cm.)

PLATE XXIV   ST AUGUSTINE IN HIS CELL Florence, Church of Ognissanti
Detail (33.5 cm.)

TE XXV   ST AUGUSTINE IN HIS CELL   Florence, Church of Ognissanti
Detail (33.5 cm.)

PLATE XXVI   MADONNA OF THE MAGNIFICAT Florence, Uffizi
Whole (diam. 118 cm.)

MADONNA OF THE MAGNIFICAT Florence, Uffizi
Details (each, 33.5 cm.)

PLATES XXVIII-XXIX   THE ADORATION OF THE MAGI Washington, National Gallery
Whole (104.2 cm.)

PLATE XXX   FRESCOES IN THE SISTINE CHAPEL Vatican
Whole (558 cm.) and detail (50 cm.) of *The Life of Moses*

FRESCOES IN THE SISTINE CHAPEL Vatican
Detail (37 cm.) of *The Life of Moses*

PLATE XXXII   FRESCOES IN THE SISTINE CHAPEL Vatican
Whole (555 cm.) and detail (98 cm.) of *The Life of Christ*

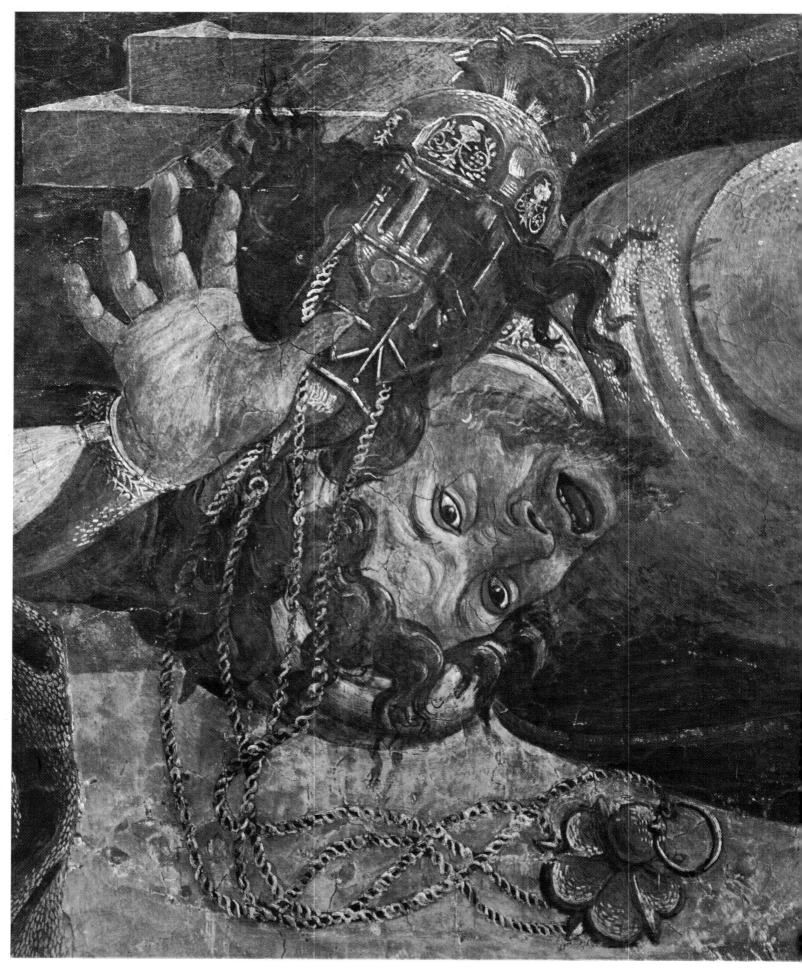

PLATE XXXIV FRESCOES IN THE SISTINE CHAPEL Vatican
Detail (41 cm.) of *The Punishment of the Rebels*

PLATES XXXVI-XXXVII   VENUS AND MARS London, National Gallery
Whole (173.5 cm.)

PLATE XXXVIII   MADONNA OF THE POMEGRANATE. Florence, Uffizi
Whole (diam. 143.5 cm.)

PORTRAIT OF A YOUNG MAN London, National Gallery
Detail (actual size)

PLATE XL   ST AUGUSTINE IN HIS CELL Florence, Uffizi
Whole (27 cm.)

PLATE XLI   DERELICTA Rome, Rospigliosi Collection
Whole (41 cm.)

PLATE XLII   ST BARNABAS ALTARPIECE   Florence, Uffizi
Whole (280 cm.) of *The Madonna and Child Enthroned with Four Angels and Six Saints*

PLATES XLIV-XLV   THE BIRTH OF VENUS Florence, Uffizi
Whole (278.5 cm.)

PLATE XLVI THE BIRTH OF VENUS Florence, Uffizi
Detail (actual size)

THE BIRTH OF VENUS Florence, Uffizi
Detail (actual size)

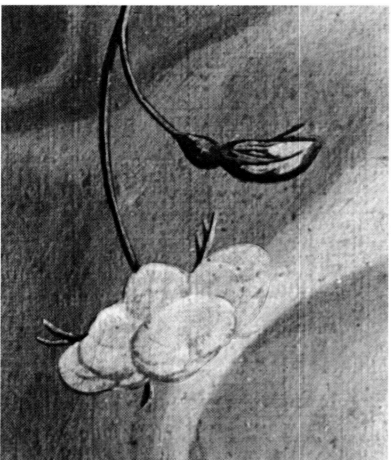

PLATE XLVIII   THE BIRTH OF VENUS Florence, Uffizi
Details (all actual size)

PLATE L　　THE ANNUNCIATION　Florence, Uffizi
Whole (156 cm.)

PLATE LI   THE ANNUNCIATION Florence, Uffizi
Detail (47.5 cm.)

THE CALUMNY OF APELLES Florence, Uffizi
Whole (91 cm.)

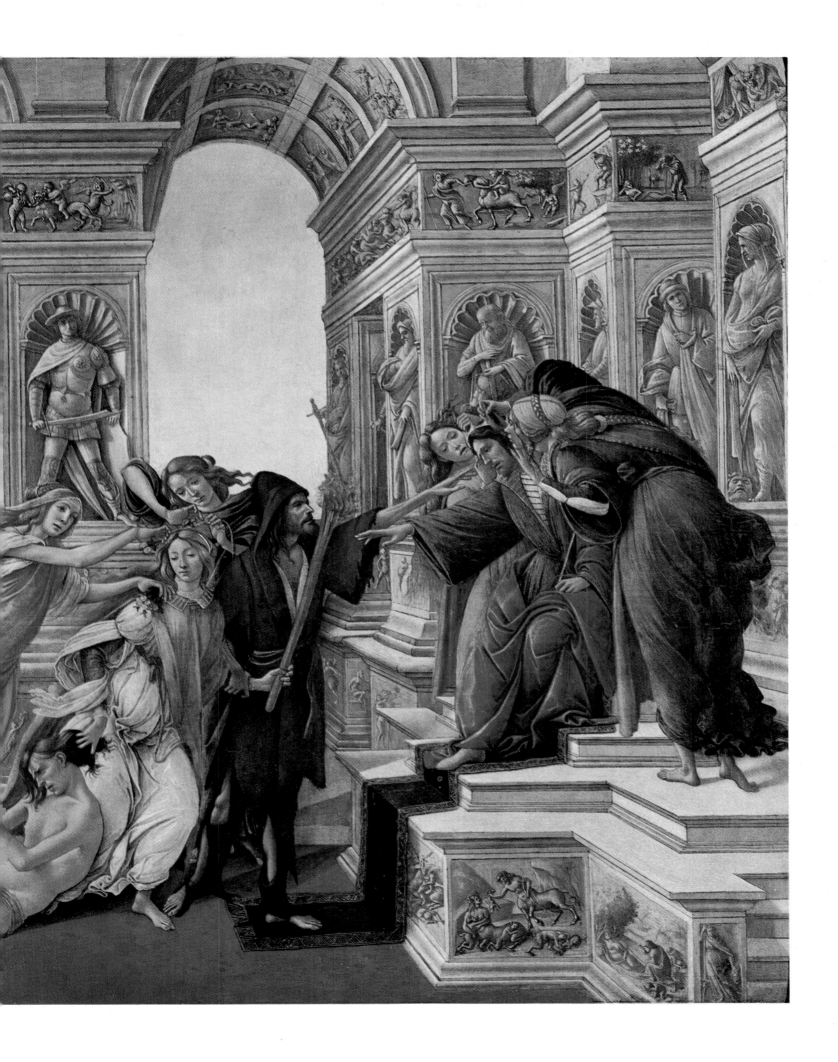

PLATE LIV   THE CALUMNY OF APELLES Florence, Uffizi
Detail (actual size)

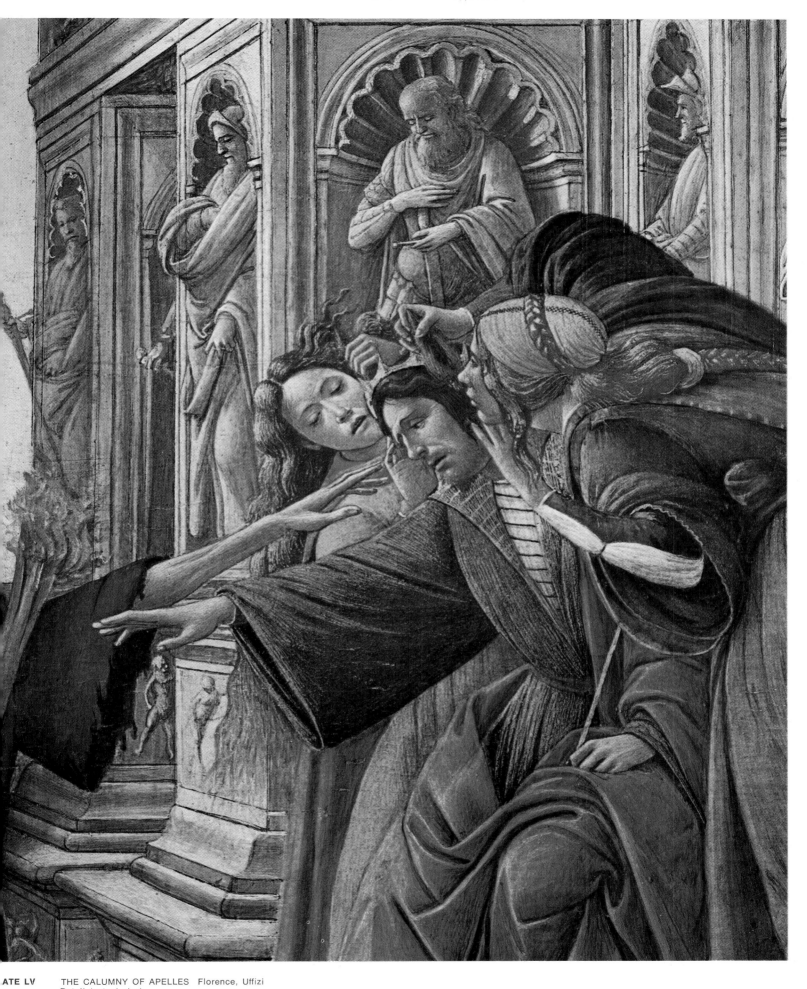

PLATE LVI   MADONNA UNDER A BALDACHIN Milan, Pinacoteca Ambrosiana
Whole (diam. 65 cm.)

LUCRETIA Boston, Isabella Stewart Gardner Museum
Detail (71 cm.)

PLATE LVIII PIETÀ Milan, Museo Poldi Pezzoli
Whole (71 cm.)

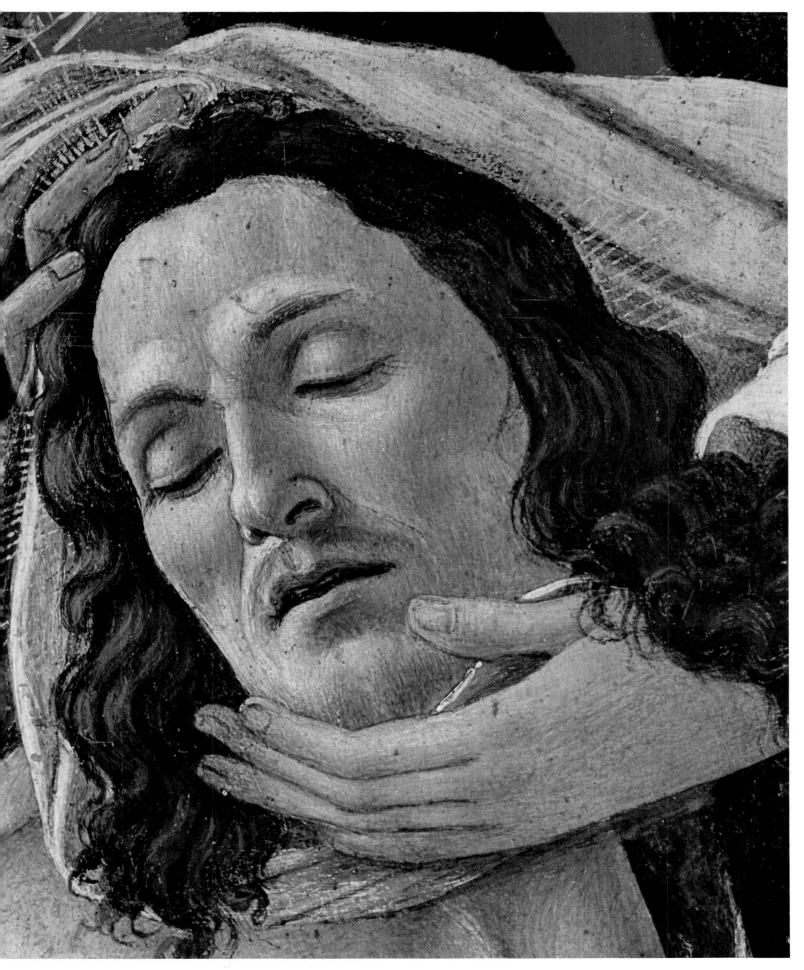

PIETA Milan, Museo Poldi Pezzoli
Detail (10.5 cm.)

PLATE LX   BARDI MADONNA   Berlin, Staatliche Museen
Details (each, 43 cm.)

PLATE LXI BARDI MADONNA Berlin, Staatliche Museen
Detail (87 cm.)

PLATE LXII   THE MYSTIC NATIVITY London, National Gallery
Whole (75 cm.)

THE MYSTIC NATIVITY London, National Gallery
Detail (25 cm.)

PLATE LXIV   THE MYSTIC NATIVITY London, National Gallery
Detail (actual size)

The Works

Key to symbols used

So that the essential elements in each work may be immediately apparent, each commentary is headed first by a number (following the most reliable chronological sequence) which is given every time that the work is quoted throughout the book, and then by a series of symbols. These refer to:
1) its execution, that is, to the degree to which it is autograph.
2) its technique.
3) its support.
4) its present whereabouts.
5) The following additional data: whether the work is signed, dated; if its present-day form is complete; if it is a finished work.

Of the other two numbers in each heading, the upper numbers refer to the picture's measurements in centimeters (height and width); the lower numbers to its date. When the date itself cannot be given with certainty, and is therefore only approximate, it is followed or preceded by an asterisk, according to whether the uncertainty relates to the period before the date given, the subsequent period, or both. All the information given corresponds to the current opinion of modern art historians; any seriously different opinions and any further clarification is mentioned in the text.

Execution

⊞ Autograph

▨ with assistance

⊞ in collaboration

⊞ with extensive collaboration

⊞ from his workshop

⊞ currently attributed

⊞ currently rejected

⊠ traditionally attributed

⊠ recently attributed

Technique

⊕ Oil

⊕ Fresco

⊕ Tempera

Support

⊕ Wood

⊕ Plaster

⊕ Canvas

Whereabouts

⦂ Public Collection

⦂ Private Collection

⦂ Unknown

⦂ Lost

Additional Data

▤ Signed

▤ Dated

▤ Incomplete or fragment

▤ Unfinished

⊞⊕▤ Symbols given in the text

Bibliography

The literature on Botticelli, albeit vast (the best summary is in Yashiro's monograph), can be restricted to the following entries and does not include popularizing texts. Documentary works, in addition to F. ALBERTINI (*Memoriale*, Florence, 1510), the so-called *Libro* of A. BILLI (1516–30; Berlin, 1892, ed. C. Frey), the ANONIMO GADDIANO (c. 1540; *id.*) and G. VASARI (*Le vite*, Florence, 1550 and 1568), include: E. MÜNTZ (*Les Collections des Médicis*, Paris, 1895), E. STEINMANN (*Die sixtinische Kapelle*, Munich, 1901–5), D. GNOLI (*Archivio storico dell'arte*, 1892), G. B. CAVALCASELLE and J. A. CROWE (*Storia della pittura italiana*, Florence, 1894), E. MÜLLER-WALDE (*Jahrbuch der preussischen Kunstsammlungen*, 1897), I. B. SUPINO (*Botticelli*, Florence, 1900), G. POGGI (*L'arte*, 1902, and *Burlington Magazine*, 1915), J. MESNIL (*Miscellanea d'arte*, 1903), H. HORNE (*Alessandro Filipepi, Commonly Called Sandro Botticelli*, London, 1908), P. BACCI (*Rivista d'arte*, 1917–18). Of the more complete monographs it is worth mentioning, in addition to Horne's work, mentioned above, those of: H. ULMANN (*Sandro Botticelli*, Munich, 1893), W. BODE (*Botticelli*, Berlin, 1921, and Leipzig, 1926), A. SCHMARSOW (*Sandro del Botticello*, Dresden, 1923), Y. YASHIRO (*Sandro Botticelli*, London and Boston, 1925 and 1929), A. VENTURI (*Botticelli*, Rome, 1925), C. GAMBA (*Botticelli*, Milan, 1936), L. VENTURI (*Botticelli*, Paris, 1937, Vienna, 1949, and London, 1961), J. MESNIL (*Botticelli*, Paris, 1938), S. BETTINI (*Botticelli*, Bergamo, 1942, 1948), G. C. ARGAN (*Botticelli*, Geneva, Paris, and New York, 1957), R. SALVINI (*Tutta la pittura del Botticelli*, Milan, 1958; "Botticelli," *Encyclopedia of World Art*,

New York, 1958–68). Among general works worth mentioning are: R. VAN MARLE (*The Development of the Italian Schools of Painting*, XII, The Hague, 1931), B. BERENSON (*Italian Pictures of the Renaissance*, Oxford, 1932, 1953, and 1968). Regarding Botticelli's portraits, of particular interest are: H. T. KROEBER (*Die Einzelporträts des Sandro Botticelli*, Leipzig, 1911), J. ALAZARD (*Le portrait florentin de Botticelli à Bronzino*, Paris, 1924, English edition, 1948), and J. POPE-HENNESSY (*The Portrait in the Renaissance*, London and New York, 1966); on color: N. ALLAN PATILLO (*Art Bulletin*, 1954); on allegorical and ideological subjects, in addition to the monographs of Argan and Salvini already cited: A. WARBURG (*Sandro Botticelli Geburt des Venus und Frühling*, Leipzig, 1893), E. JACOBSEN (*Archivio storico dell'arte*, 1897), C. R. POST (*Art in America*, 1914), R. PICCOLI (*Burlington Magazine*, 1930), R. WITTKOWER (*Journal of the Warburg and Courtauld Institutes*, 1938–9), E. H. GOMBRICH (*Ibid.*, 1945), E. WIND (*Burlington Magazine*, 1950, and *Pagan Mysteries of the Renaissance*, London, 1958), and P. FRANCASTEL (*Peinture et Société: Naissance et destruction d'un Espace Plastique de la Renaissance au Cubisme*, Lyons, 1951); on relationships with ancient art: E. TIETZE-CONRAT (*Burlington Magazine*, 1925) and R. SALVINI (*Emporium*, 1943). Concerning Botticelli's drawings, works of fundamental importance are: B. BERENSON (*The Drawings of the Florentine Painters*, Chicago, 1903 and 1938), A. VENTURI (*Il Botticelli interprete di Dante*, Milan, 1921), and A. BERTINI (*Drawings by Botticelli*, New York, 1968).

Outline biography

1445 Alessandro, called Sandro, is born to Mariano di Vanni di Amedeo Filipepi, fifty, leather tanner, and his wife, Smeralda, forty, in Florence, in Via Nuova (now Via del Porcellana), in the Ognissanti quarter, in a house next door to that of the Vespuccis.

1447 1 MARCH In a document of this year, his father declares that Alessandro is two years old. The Filipepis now live in Via della Vigna Nuova in a house belonging to the Rucellais. The family tannery is on the other side of the Arno River near the Santa Trinita bridge.

1458 28 FEBRUARY In a legal document Mariano Filipepi, sixty-five, states that he has four sons: Giovanni, thirty-seven and married; Antonio, a goldsmith, twenty-eight; Simone, fourteen, an apprentice of Paolo Rucellai, a cloth merchant in Naples; Sandro, thirteen, who "reads and is unhealthy." There is some doubt about the proper interpretation of this phrase, for the Italian verb *legere* is argued by some to mean "alloy" and could mean that Sandro worked for a goldsmith with the specific function of preparing alloys. Those students who read the word as "to read" argue that the contemporary spelling of the verb "to alloy" would be *leghare*, not *legere*. According to Vasari (1550), Sandro's father "placed him with a goldsmith, a friend called Botticello, who was very skilled in the art." Scholars have rejected the theory of such an apprenticeship on the grounds that there is no other mention of a goldsmith of that name. It has more commonly been supposed that the name "Botticelli" derived from the nickname applied to Sandro's older brother Giovanni, who was so fat that he was called "Botticella," the tub. But this theory is not supported by contemporary evidence. Thus one comes to a hypothesis that would be in accord with Vasari. Antonio, another brother of Sandro, was a goldsmith and is cited as "a beater of gold," which is to say a *battigello* in the workshop parlance of the fifteenth century. Perhaps, then, this is the origin of the nickname applied to both brothers, in which case it is possible that Sandro worked with his gold-smith brother before entering the workshop of Fra Filippo Lippi. In fact, Sandro was rather old, in terms of contemporary practice, when he entered that artist's workshop. Even in Sandro's lifetime the term *battigello* had been deformed to *botticella*.

1464c Sandro entered the workshop of Fra Filippo Lippi, perhaps on the recommendation of the Vespuccis. Sandro remained at least until 1467. This information, from Vasari, is supported by a series of works by Lippi in which Botticelli's hand can be detected. Some believe they have identified Botticelli's contributions in Lippi's last frescoes in Prato.

1467 In Neri di Bicci's *Libro*, mention is made of Sandro's brother Antonio, described as a gilder. It is possible that, after Lippi's departure for Spoleto, Botticelli continued the work-shop, finishing commissions that had already been started, or that he went to Verrocchio's workshop. Another hypothesis that has been advanced is that Verrocchio was already working with Lippi, and that immediately after Lippi's departure, he opened a workshop with Sandro. It is suggested that Verrocchio left the responsibility for painted work to Sandro (though under the former's direction) and devoted himself to the management of sculptural and goldsmith's work. (See also **1469**.)

1469 Legal declaration by Mariano Filipepi (Florence, *Archivio delle decime*) in which he states that Sandro, twenty-three, works at home. The family then consisted of fifteen members and, thanks in part to a legacy, possessed arable lands, vineyards, and shops. Filippo Lippi died in Spoleto on 9 October.

1470 Botticelli had his own workshop in Florence, according to Benedetto Dei's *Ricordanze:* "a workshop of Maestro Sandro Batticello, Florentine" (Florence, Biblioteca Riccardiana). Between 18 June, the date the commission was confirmed, and 18 August, the date on which final payment was made, Botticelli painted *Fortitude* for the tribunal of the Merchants' Guild (*Catalogue* 26). He had this first documented official commission thanks to the new consul of the guild, Tommaso Soderini, one of the Medicis' men. A second panel, likewise commissioned for the tribunal, was never executed, perhaps because of the protestations of Piero del Pollaiuolo, who had been commissioned to paint all seven Virtues in 1469.

(Left) Probable self-portrait of Botticelli in The Adoration of the Magi *(Florence, Uffizi). (Right) Presumed portrait of Botticelli in Filippino Lippi's fresco with Saints Peter and Paul before the Proconsul (Florence, Carmine, Brancacci Chapel).*

1472 18 OCTOBER Botticelli joined the Compagnia degli artisti di San Luca, paying the chamberlain, Andrea della Robbia, six *soldi* for admission, five for annual dues, and five *soldi* and four *denari* for his workshop. Then Filippino Lippi, fifteen, was admitted as an apprentice: "Filippo di Filippo da Prato, painter with Sandro di Botticello," according to the *Libro rosso de' debitori e creditori* of the guild. Likewise mentioned in the *Libro rosso* is Sandro's brother Antonio as a gilder and goldsmith.

1473 The *Libro rosso* of the guild records other payments made by Sandro.

1474 20 JANUARY On the feast of St Sebastian, Sandro's *St Sebastian* was solemnly installed on a pillar of the nave of Sta Maria Maggiore in Florence, according to the Anonimo Gaddiano. The painting is identified with the one now in Berlin (*Catalogue*, 39). On 24 January, Sandro was summoned to Pisa to discuss the frescoes to be painted at the Camposanto, alongside the eight already painted by Gozzoli. ("He came from Florence to see where he would have to paint in the Camposanto, about 27 January, Pisa Cathedral, *Libro delle ricordanze*.) It was agreed that he must demonstrate his ability, so he agreed to paint an *Assumption of the Virgin* for the cathedral. He worked from July to 20 September without completing the work. ("Sandro, called Botticello, painter … [received payment] for the painting of a scene begun in the Incoronata Chapel of the Cathedral, a painting of the Assumption of Our Lady, which work he undertakes for purposes of comparison and, if pleasing, he has then to paint in the Camposanto" [Opera del Duomo di Pisa, *Libro delle entrate e uscite*]). The unfinished fresco was destroyed in 1583. It is not known why Sandro never painted in the Camposanto.

1475 28 JANUARY A joust was held in Piazza Sta Croce, Florence, and many artists took part in the decoration. Giuliano de' Medici had a standard painted by Botticelli. This standard, described in a Magliabechio codex, is mentioned among the Medici possessions in a document prepared at the death of Lorenzo the Magnificent. According to the Anonimo Gaddiano, Botticelli painted near the Porta della Catena in the Palazzo della Signoria, at the top of the outer staircase of the courtyard, an *Adoration of the Magi*. This was destroyed during Vasari's remodeling of the palace.

1478 Between 26 April, the date of the Pazzi Conspiracy, and 21 July, the date of payment, Sandro painted on the Porta della Dogana (which faces Via de' Gondi, in Palazzo Vecchio) the conspirators hanged by the neck: Jacopo, Francesco and Renato de' Pazzi, and Archbishop Salviati. The escaped conspirators were depicted hanging by a foot. The paintings were removed on 14 November, 1494, after the flight of Piero de' Medici.

1480 On commission by the Vespuccis, he painted in the Church of Ognissanti in Florence, the fresco of St Augustine (*Catalogue*, 60), in competition with Ghirlandaio. According to a document of the time the Filepepi family now owned the house next to the one they lived in. In a legal document Botticelli declared the following assistants: Raffaello di Lorenzo di Frosino Tosi, born in 1469; Giovanni di Benedetto Cianfanini, eighteen, unsalaried; Jacopo di Domenico Papi, paid eighteen florins. Elsewhere Sandro mentioned an assistant named Ludovico.

1481 In January, in a legal document, Mariano declares: "Sandro di Mariano, thirty-five years of age, is a painter and works at home when and as he will." Because of the legal script of the time, it is hard to tell if the figure 35 is not, in fact, 33. Between April and May Sandro frescoed *The Annunciation* at San Martino alla Scala to adorn the wall of the tomb of Cione Pollini, the founder of the hospice (*Catalogue*, 62). Then he went to Rome, where, with other painters, he painted a trial fresco for the Sistine Chapel on the commission of Pope Sixtus IV. As a result of that trial, a contract was drawn up on 27 October, according to which Cosimo Rosselli, Ghirlandaio, Perugino and Botticelli agreed each to carry out his own part in the work, with suitable help, by 15 March 1482 (minute in *Archivio Segreto Vaticano*).

1482 17 FEBRUARY The payment for individual frescoes for the Sistine Chapel walls was set at 250 gold ducats. Meanwhile, the number of scenes to be painted was increased, and additional painters were summoned: Signorelli, Pinturicchio and Piero di Cosimo. Painted by

Sandro were the second and fifth section of the left wall and the second section of the right wall. With extensive collaboration by assistants, from eleven to fourteen figures of popes between the window arches can be ascribed to Sandro (*Catalogue* 63, A–N). On 20 February Sandro's father died; he was buried in Ognissanti. On 5 October, in the presence of the painters, the Operai del Palazzo della Signoria drew up an agreement in Florence with Botticelli, Perugino, Piero del Pollaiuolo and Biagio d'Antonio Tucci for the fresco decoration of the Sala dei Gigli (or Sala dei Priori). Botticelli's task, together with Ghirlandaio (the general director of the work), was the wall toward the Sala delle Udienze. The only fresco that was executed was a *St Zenobius* by Ghirlandaio. On 25 November Sandro paid ten *soldi* to the Compagnia di San Luca.

1483 On commission from Lorenzo the Magnificent, Sandro painted, with extensive collaboration of his assistants, the four *cassone* panels depicting episodes from Nastagio degli Onesti's story in the *Decameron*, on the occasion of the marriage of Giannozzo Pucci with Lucrezia di Piero di Giovanni Bini (*Catalogue* 74, A–D). Filippino Lippi, who had been working independently for some time, depicted Sandro among the witnesses in *The Martyrdom of St Peter* in the Brancacci Chapel of the Church of the Carmine in Florence. Perhaps in 1483, or 1484 at the latest, Sandro competed – along with Filippino Lippi, Perugino, and Ghirlandaio – for Lorenzo the Magnificent's decoration of the Villa dello Spedaletto in Volterra (*Catalogue* 79). This information appears in a letter directed to Ludovico il Moro from an unknown agent

[Müller-Walde, 1889] (see also *Critical Outline*), which appears to have been written about 1485 and to refer to events that have taken place recently.

1485 AUGUST Paid by Agnolo Bardi for *The Madonna and Child between the two Saints John*, painted for the altar of the Bardi Chapel in Sto Spirito (*Catalogue* 87). Giuliano da Sangallo had received a payment in February for the frame of this panel.

1487 The magistrate of the Massai di Camera commissioned a *tondo* for the audience hall of his magistrature in Palazzo Vecchio: The work may be identified as *The Madonna of the Pomegranate* (*Catalogue,* 89).

1488–90 He painted *The Annunciation* for the Church of Sta Maria Maddalena de' Pazzi, then the church of the monks of Cestello. A contemporary document (see *Catalogue* 102) published by Milanesi, records "on 19 March [Florentine calendar, hence 1489] Benedetto di ser Giovanni Guardi had a chapel made in Cestello in Florence … and spent for the panel in that chapel 30 ducats, a work done by the hand of Sandro Botticelli."

1490 13 OCTOBER In the *Libro* of the officers of the *Notte e Monasteri* is the entry *Sander Botticelli fecit contra ordinamenta*. There is no record of what kind of infraction this referred to.

1491 5 JANUARY He was summoned along with Lorenzo di Credi, Ghirlandaio, Perugino and Alessio Baldovinetti to join a commission to judge the projects submitted for the

façade of Florence cathedral. On 18 May the Opera del Duomo commissioned him to do the mosaic decoration, with Gherardo and Monte di Giovanni, of two spandrels of the vault of the Chapel of S. Zanobi. The other two spandrels were commissioned of the Ghirlandaio brothers. Botticelli received payment for these works on 25 August, 13 December, and finally 18 December 1492; but he never completed the work. That was done by Davide Ghirlandaio and Monte di Giovanni.

1493 30 MARCH His elder brother Giovanni died and was buried in the Church of Ognissanti. His brother Simone returned from Naples and lived with Sandro.

1494 19 APRIL With his brother Simone he bought a villa and farm outside Porta San Frediano: "a gentleman's house at San Sepolcro in Bellosguardo with twelve *staiora* of vineyards. We bought it for 156 gross florins … on 19 April" (registered by Simone Filipepi; Florence, State Archives). But he actually settled with his nephews Benincasa and Lorenzo in the Sta Maria Novella quarter, perhaps in his parents' house, where he was born.

1495 25 NOVEMBER The wife of Lorenzo di Pierfrancesco de' Medici wrote in a letter that Botticelli was expected at the villa in Trebbio to "paint some things for Lorenzo." About this time Medici commissioned the painter to illustrate *The Divine Comedy* (see *Appendix*).

1496 14 JUNE, 7 and 20 JULY, 14 AUGUST He received payments in full for a *St Francis* painted – perhaps in fresco – for the dormitory of Sta Maria di Monticelli outside Porta San Frediano: the building was destroyed at the time of the siege of 1529–30. On 2 July Michelangelo Buonarroti wrote from Rome, to "Sandro di Botticelli in Florence," a letter for Lorenzo di Pierfrancesco de' Medici, then unwelcome in Florence and all but confined to his villa in Trebbio.

1497 2 JULY The administrator of Lorenzo di Pierfrancesco de' Medici acknowledged a credit to Sandro Botticelli for decorations painted with assistants in the Medici villa at Castello. From an account sent on 3 July to Leonardo Strozzi in Florence, it appears that workmen and decorators worked in the villa for Botticelli. More than three hundred Florentine supporters of Savonarola signed a petition asking the pope to rescind the friar's excommunication. Botticelli did not sign the petition, although according to contemporary critics he must have shared Savonarola's ideas.

1498 Botticelli declared before the tax office that he resided with his brother Simone in the

house of his nephews Benincasa and Lorenzo in the Sta Maria Novella quarter. The earnings of the Bellosguardo property outside Porta San Frediano were declared to total 156 large florins. On 18 February, under the guarantee of one Antonio di Migliore Guidotti, Sandro Botticelli and the cobbler Filippo di Domenico del Cavaliere, his neighbor at Bellosguardo, exchanged notarized reciprocal promises no longer to offend each other. On 15 March, Guidantonio Vespucci, having bought a house in Via de' Servi, called in to decorate it Piero di Cosimo and Botticelli, who, according to Vasari, "painted all around the room several pictures with vivid and beautiful figures framed in walnut for bench-backs and woodwork." Perhaps these were the scenes

Presumed self-portrait of Botticelli in The Punishment of the Rebels *(Vatican, Sistine Chapel). Some have thought there was also a self-portrait in* The Life of Christ, *in the first figure in the left foreground; this suggestion, advanced by Gebhardt and accepted by some scholars, including Geffroy, has had no confirmation.*

of Virginia and Lucretia (*Catalogue* 144, A and B). On 29 May Savonarola was burned at the stake in Piazza della Signoria. On 20 September Luca Pacioli's *Summa de arithmetica, geometria, proportioni et proportionalità* was published in Venice. In that work Botticelli is mentioned as an able master of perspective, along with Filippino Lippi and Ghirlandaio.

1499 2 NOVEMBER Simone Filipepi wrote in his *Cronaca*: "Alessandro di Mariano Filipepi, my brother, one of the fine painters that our city has had in these times, did, in my presence, being at home by the fire about the third hour of the night, relate how that day, in his workshop at Sandro's house, he had discussed with Doffo Spini the question of Brother Girolamo [Savonarola]"; Spini had been one of the leading judges in the trial of Savonarola. On 15 November Botticelli paid the matriculation fee in the reorganized Guild of *Medici e Speziali*, which also included painters.

1501 JANUARY He completed *The Mystic Nativity* (*Catalogue* 148), the only known painting by Botticelli that is signed and dated.

1502 23 SEPTEMBER Francesco de' Malatesta wrote to Isabella d'Este, whose agent he was, that Perugino, whom the Duchess of Ferrara wanted to commission to finish the paintings in her *studiolo* (left incomplete by Mantegna), was in Siena and that Filippino Lippi, to whom he had then turned, was too busy, but that "another, Alexandro Botechiella, has been much recommended to me as an excellent painter and a man who works happily and is not occupied as are the afore-mentioned. He was approached and says that he would undertake the commission and happily serve your Ladyship." It seems likely then that Botticelli was free of commissions at the time. On 16 November Botticelli was charged with sodomy, but it would seem that no legal action resulted. In Florence at the time charges of this kind were rather common.

1503 In the poem *De illustratione urbis Florentiae*, Ugolino Verino mentions as famous painters Giotto, Taddeo Gaddi, Pollaiuolo, Filippino Lippi, Domenico and Davide Ghirlandaio, Leonardo da Vinci and Botticelli, whom he compares to Zeuxis and Apelles. From this year until 1505, Botticelli was in arrears in his fees to the Compagnia di San Luca.

1504 25 JANUARY Together with Giuliano da Sangallo, Cosimo Rosselli, Leonardo da Vinci, Filippino Lippi and Bernardo Bandinelli (Baccio's father), he was a member of the commission charged with designing the setting for Michelangelo's *David*. Botticelli, together with Giuliano da Sangallo and Cosimo Rosselli, proposed the steps of the Cathedral. Preference was given to the proposal of Filippino Lippi and Michelangelo himself, and the statue was set up in Piazza della Signoria in front of Palazzo Comunale.

1505 18 OCTOBER Botticelli settles his debts to the Compagnia di San Luca.

1510 17 MAY According to the *Libro dei morti* of the city of Florence and of his guild, Botticelli was buried in the cemetery of the Church of Ognissanti. The many vicissitudes of the cemetery and church have resulted in various relocations of graves. Botticelli's grave lies beneath an area adjacent to the railing of the Chapel of S. Pietro d'Alcantara, which was built in 1722. A marble *tondo* has been set over the grave with the Filipepi bearings: a lion rampant turned left. In the front right paw is a half-open pair of compasses with the points up.

SANDRO BOTTICELLI PITT. FIORENTINO

Depiction of Botticelli preceding his biography in Vasari's Vite *(Florence, 1568)*

84

Catalogue of works

From the preceding (*Critical outline and Outline biography*) it seems fairly evident what the stylistic development of the young Botticelli was; from the gay opulence of color, marked by subtlety of line – so poetically allusive rather than vigorously naturalistic – of Fra Filippo Lippi; to the very plastic and terse outlines of Pollaiuolo; to the punctilious finishing of Verrocchio. The influence of the first two masters must have provided the basis of the timbre of Platonic idealism peculiar to the early Botticelli and of his very eclectic sense of decoration. For this reason critics have compared him to the Sienese painters, particularly Simone Martini, and to the miniaturists of the Far East. One can accept this up to a point, but one should give this no more weight than one would to calling Botticelli one of the "fathers" of Art Nouveau, a suggestion that is only justifiable by way of his influence on the pre-Raphaelite movement. What the example of Verrocchio may have done was to loosen Botticelli's line and make it more articulate, to give it a more vibrant sense of melody, albeit solidly volumetric, fully aware of space and perspective.

With the assimilation of these elements into his idiom, the artistic personality of Botticelli was complete. Action is suspended in contemplation, reality becomes a dream of beauties traced out in a translucent atmosphere that is ever lighter: a dream, a myth. But subsequent political events – in particular, the advent of Savonarola (the attraction of whose sermons for Botticelli is as demonstrable as the earlier influence of Medicean neo-Platonism) – caused a profound change in Botticelli: dream and absorbed contemplation become mystical imploring; myth becomes a tragic allegory of a humanity deprived of justice. And slowly the figures tend to become enclosed in ever tighter formal shapes. At the same time there is a severe cooling of compositional schemata in a supremely lyrical unity.

As for the technique employed in his easel work, Botticelli remained faithful to what is called "egg tempera." He brought the technique to perfection. His favorite support was panel, usually walnut. He very rarely painted on canvas. The preparation of the surface to be painted was composed of "white of Spain" and "white color" in powder form, bound with a comparable weight of carpenter's glue (about 80 grams per liter of water). This mixture was laid on in crossed layers so thin that seven or eight of them are scarcely more than one millimeter thick. Perspective lines and architecture, etc., were incised on the preparation with a stylus. The rest was outlined with a brush in a liquid brown tint. Color was applied in successive separate layers – particularly in the final transparent layers – with a "varnish" of Pergamene glue. The backgrounds (landscapes, etc.) and the final translucent layers were, in his late works, applied in casein tempera.

In his wall paintings, the drawing *(sinopia)* was carried out in broad general lines. And Botticelli must have used this typically medieval procedure throughout his career, because none of his frescoes betrays a cartoon that has been transported nor the mark of the tracing stylus (common practice by the end of the fifteenth century). The only exception was in marking out perspective lines, ornamental framing elements and such things, which had been traced out in this way even before Botticelli. The joining of the *giornate* appears to have been carefully leveled and retouched *a secco*. And various areas of his frescoed surfaces seem to have been treated this way.

According to the sources (Vasari, in particular), his pupils and, in general belief, his assistants were: Jacopo di Francesco di Domenico Filippi (?–1527), Jacopo di Domenico Papi, called Toschi

(1463–1530), Biagio d'Antonio Pucci (1446–1515), Raffaello di Lorenzo di Frosino Tosi, called Toso (1469– ?), Giovanni di Benedetto Cianfanini (1462–1542). Better known to the critics, because of evidence of their hands in various works by Botticelli, are Filippino Lippi (1457–1504), his nephew Mariano d'Antonio (c. 1400–68) – the full extent of whose collaboration is yet to be determined – Jacopo del Sellaio (1442–93) – perhaps only sporadically a collaborator but a constant imitator and copyist. It is possible that Raffaellino del Garbo (c. 1470–c. 1525) should be added to this list. A hypothetical "friend of Sandro" need not be mentioned. This figure was hypothesized but later rejected by Berenson. Among followers whose work has sometimes been confused with that of Botticelli, or more commonly with that of his workshop, mention should be made of Piero di Cosimo (1462–1521 ?), Bartolomeo di Giovanni (? – ?), Francesco di Giorgio Martini (1439–1502) in his Florentine period, and, more importantly, Francesco Botticini (1446–97 ?), who sometimes, because of his name, was confused with Botticelli. Mention should also be made of the mosaicists and miniaturists Gherardo and Monte di Giovanni, to whom some scholars attribute extensive collaboration in small-scale work by Botticelli; and Giuliano da Sangallo, who not only executed frames for Botticelli's paintings but also seems to have made pencil copies of drawings and paintings. Finally, there were many anonymous copyists and followers that continued in the manner of Botticelli long after the artist's death and after his workshop had long been producing copies. The work of these men has given critics very intricate and often insoluble problems

1 🔳 ◔ 100×71 1464* 📘 ⋮

Madonna and Child with two Angels (Havemeyer Madonna) New York, Metropolitan Museum
From the parish church of Castelfranco di Sopra (Valdarno) it went to Cerreto to the chapel of the Counts Baglioni, who sold it about 1900. It went to the Harnish

2

4
Collection, Philadelphia, then to the Havemeyers, and to its present home. For Berenson [1932] and Gamba, the first known work of Botticelli; doubtful for Mesnil; not mentioned by others. Variation – on an oval support – of a *tondo* by Filippo Lippi (to whom attributed by Colasanti [1903]), in which Sandro's hand can be seen in the angel on the right.

2 🔳 ◔ 89×60 1464* 📘 ⋮

Madonna and Child with two Angels Washington, National Gallery of Art (Samuel H. Kress Bequest) Formerly in Sedelmeyer, Paris, Brady, Long Island, and Macaulay, Washington, Collections. Attributed by Berenson [1932], accepted by Gamba, Bettini and Salvini; rejected by Mesnil [1938], not mentioned by others.

3

3 🔳 ◔ 87×60 1465* 📘 ⋮

Madonna and Child with Angel Florence, Museo dell'Ospedale degli Innocenti Variation of a work by Lippi and painted in Lippi's workshop (to whom it was attributed until Ulmann [1893] – and then many others – attributed it to Botticelli), either by Botticelli alone or with his extensive collaboration. It has suffered much by old cleanings; restored in 1890. Large areas seem to have been removed and repainted.

4 🔳 ◔ 73×40 1466* 📘 ⋮

Madonna and Child (Guidi Madonna) Paris, Louvre Formerly in the Guidi Collection, Faenza; sold in Rome in 1902 by Sangiorgi; went to the Louvre in the Schlichting bequest. A work entirely executed by Botticelli in Lippi's workshop (according to A. Venturi [1902 and 1907] and others, though some – since Jamot [1920] – attribute it to the school). It recalls the Munich *Madonna* and the *tondo* in the Pitti.

5 ⊞ ◉ 110×70 1466* ▤ ⫶

Madonna and Child with Angel Ajaccio, Corsica, Musée Fesch
Many recent critics [Vertova, 1948, up to Salvini] consider it one of the first entirely autograph works of Botticelli.

6

7

8

There is the beginning of the rhythmic lyric quality of later works.

6 ⊞ ◉ 72×52 1468* ▤ ⫶

Madonna and Child Paris, Louvre
Went to the Louvre in 1863. From 1872 it was for some time in Périgueux museum. Attributed to the Botticelli school by Berenson [1932] and

9

Pittaluga [1949], while Laclotte [1956] ascribes it to Botticelli about 1470, and Salvini to 1468, but traditionally assigned to Lippi.

7 ⊞ ◉ 85×62 1468* ▤ ⫶

Madonna and Child with Young St John and two Angels Florence, Galleria dell'Accademia
From Sta Maria Nuova, Florence, it went to the Uffizi in 1900, and was transferred to the Academia (1919). Considered autograph by almost all scholars [from Bode, 1884, to Salvini] except Horne [1908] and A. Venturi [1925], who ascribe it to the school. Motifs from Lippi and Verrocchio would be in keeping with Botticelli, particularly the finely wrought figures – among parts attributable to others – despite depressing retouching.

8 ⊞ ◉ 72×50 1468* ▤ ⫶

Infant Christ Embracing the Madonna (Madonna of the Loggia) Florence, Uffizi
Went to the Uffizi – by 1784 – from the Florence Chamber of Commerce and there was attributed to Botticelli. Rejected by Morelli [1890] and others [until Mesnil, 1938]; reascribed to Botticelli by A. Venturi [1911] and subsequently rejected [1925] by him and later scholars; again ascribed [Gamba, 1932, to Salvini]. The forms of Lippi are adapted to a more *mouvementé* setting, with echoes of Verrocchio and Baldovinetti, and perhaps of a Mantegna *Madonna* that reached Florence in 1467. Damaged, particularly the Virgin's cloak, and the

landscape seems totally repainted.

9 ⊞ ◉ 83,7×59 1468* ▤ ⫶

Madonna and Child with Young Worshipper Chicago, Max and Leola Epstein Collection
Sold after 1907 by Féral, Paris, to Van Buren, Amsterdam, then to Epstein in 1925. Autograph according to A. Venturi [1907], Yashiro, Bode [1926] and Van Marle, but for Gamba and Salvini it is a workshop copy. Undoubtedly painted after *The Madonna of the Loggia* (8), but the design and line are sharper. The left side is slightly damaged, and the Madonna's robe has been altered.

10 ⊞ ◉ 93×69 1468* ▤ ⫶

Madonna and Child with Young St John (Madonna of the Rosebush) Paris, Louvre
Acquired in 1824 by Louis XVIII. Related to Botticelli by Cavalcaselle and confirmed by Ulmann [1893]. A work of sure, high quality; some scholars date it as late as 1472 [Yashiro, to L. Venturi, 1937], while most date it between 1468 and 1469 because of the influence of Lippi's spirit and the growing influence of Verrocchio. The background leaves do not yet show the mixture of black and yellow (Pompeian green) thickly spread that characterizes Botticelli's later work. Retouched as early as 1490, and unglazed at several points.

11 ⊞ ◉ 74×56 1468* ▤ ⫶

Madonna and Child (Corsini Madonna) Washington, National Gallery of Art (Mellon Bequest)
From the Corsini's gallery in Florence, it passed to Duveen, N.Y., then to the Mellon Collection, Washington. There old repainting was removed and Botticelli's delicacy [Bode, 1893; etc.], still influenced by Lippi, was revealed. The painting was once attributed to Filippino Lippi. Verrocchio's influence is also clearly present.

12 ⊞ ◉ 168×112 1468* ▤ ⫶

Madonna Enthroned Settignano (Florence), Cappella della Vannella

12

13

14

15

16

Drastically altered by numerous repaintings, slight original traces survive in the outlines of faces. One can still see the composition of Botticelli, as all modern scholars agree [Horne, 1901, etc.], dating it about 1468.

13 ⊞ ◉ 70×48 1468* ▤ ⫶

Madonna and Child with Angel London, National Gallery
Disposed of by the Zambrinis of Imola in 1857. Although questioned by most scholars [Cavalcaselle to Davies, 1951], it may be attributed, according to Mesnil and Salvini, to Botticelli at the time he abandoned the manner of Lippi for the forms of Verrocchio.

14 ⊞ ◉ 100×71 1468 - 69 ▤ ⫶

Madonna and Child with two Angels Naples, Gallerie Nazionali di Capodimonte
It was in Palazzo Farnese, Rome, from 1697, curiously catalogued as by "Fra' Filippino." Attributed to Botticelli by most scholars. The mixture of elements of Lippi and Verrocchio suggests execution between 1468 and 1469. Almost totally repainted. Restored in 1957.

15 ⊞ ◉ 107×75 1469* ▤ ⫶

Madonna and Child with two Angels Strasbourg, Musée des Beaux-Arts
Attributed to Botticelli by Bode [1921] and largely followed [to Salvini]; rejected by Berenson and Mesnil. Freer in layout and composition than earlier works, it seems to assimilate all influences with a subtle wealth of detail. Christ's pose is characteristic of the later Botticelli. Much retouched; the Madonna's face is much damaged.

16 ⊞ ◉ 69,5×50 1469* ▤ ⫶

Madonna and Child with two Angels London, National Gallery
From the Callcott Collection (acquired in the middle of the nineteenth century), then in the Davenport, Bromley, Fairfax Murray, and other Collections until, with the Salting Bequest, it entered the National Gallery (1910). Scholars disagree (ascribed to Pesellino by Waagen [1857]; then to Lippi, and finally Botticelli, according to Ulmann [1893]; challenged by Bode [1926] and others; but supported by Gamba [1932] and most moderns). The compactness of plan and color are stronger than in any other work of the young Botticelli. Verrocchio himself or one of his close associates may have had a hand in the

17

18

repainted, so that it is hard to judge the whole work, which seems ill-composed and rather heavy. There remain, however, Botticellian traces (noted by Bode [1887] and accepted eventually by most modern critics [Schmarsow, 1923, to Salvini]) close to *Fortitude* (26) with its elements of Pollaiuolo.

19 ⊞ ◑ 53,3×36,2 1469* 目 ⦂

Portrait of a Young Man
Santa Monica, California,
Barbara Hutton Collection
Exhibited in 1886 at the Royal
Academy, London, as a work by
Fiorenzo di Lorenzo. Formerly
in the Heart Collection, New
York, it was connected to
Botticelli by Gamba and
Salvini (and ignored by
others), but the attribution was
Berenson's [1932]. The sky and
landscape echo an iconography
then brought into vogue by
Baldovinetti and immediately
assimilated by Pollaiuolo. The
same handling of the sky can be
noted in later works of

work, particularly in the haloes
(especially that of the Madonna,
which is so polished that it
reflects the back of her neck),
the punctilious metallic
quality of the garments of the
angel on the left, and the sharp
outline of the trees.

17 ⧆ ◑ 177×151 目 ⦂

The Baptism of Christ
Florence, Uffizi
This work, traditionally
ascribed to Verrocchio, with
the well-known collaboration
of the young Leonardo, was
reassigned to Botticelli by
Ragghianti [1954], because of
stylistic elements and because
of the absence of evidence of
Verrocchio's activity as a
painter. Consequently the
problem was raised of attributing
to Sandro other works hitherto
attributed to Verrocchio. It is
possible that at the beginning
of his career, Botticelli was in
Verrocchio's workshop,
executing along with other
collaborators, including
Leonardo, works for which
Verrocchio was merely the
organiser. Nevertheless most
scholars refuse to admit this
and similar works to Botticelli's
canon — because there is no
documentary evidence and
because of certain technical
details, e.g., the addition of oil
to the egg tempera, impasto
with shaded layers and thick
varnishes, none of which were
ever employed by Botticelli.
Ragghianti's opinion should be
borne in mind, however, until
further judgment can be made
on the basis of direct comparison
of all the works.

18 ⊞ ◑ 62×42 1469* 目 ⦂

**Madonna and Child with
five Angels** Paris, Louvre
This painting, still in its original
frame, has been extensively

Botticelli, such as *Portrait of a
Man* (41).

20 ⊞ ◑ 51×33,7 1469* 目 ⦂

Portrait of a Young Man
Florence, Pitti
A. Venturi's attribution to
Botticelli in 1891 (formerly
ascribed to Andrea del
Castagno) was long challenged;
reconfirmed by Gamba [1932
and 1936] and others
[Rusconi, 1937; Bettini, 1942;
Collobi Ragghianti, 1949;
Ciaranfi Francini, 1956], and
now generally accepted. Bode's
dating to c. 1475 [1921] (and
later [1926] to 1480–5) was
generally challenged in favor
of c. 1470. Despite the cleaning
in 1935, the picture is still much
darker than other works of
Botticelli. This may have been
due to a later treatment of the
tempera rather than to an
attempt by the artist to employ
Flemish techniques.

21 ⊞ ◑ 目 °°

Portrait of a Young Man
Formerly Naples, Museo
Filangieri

19

22

20

21

23

The attribution in the inventories
was justly rejected by Kroeber
[1911]. The static quality of the
figure suggests [Van Marle] an
imitation of the similar
Portrait of a Young Man in the
Pitti (20). Lost in the twentieth
century.

22 ⊞ ◑ *52×33* 目 ⦂

Portrait of a Man New York,
Duveen Property
Yashiro [1925] considers it
autograph. Other scholars do
not, despite vague qualities of
Botticelli.

23 ⊞ ◑ 70×250* 目 ⦂

Madonna and Child Florence,
Church of Santissima
Annunziata
Fragment of fresco once in the
Chapel of the Madonna degli
Angeli adjoining the church.

25

The chapel was transformed
into a sacristy, and a door was
cut in the wall bearing this
fresco. The fragment was set
over the door. The drapery is
almost totally original. The
Madonna is damaged, and the
Child is completely repainted.
Insufficient evidence to
accept Gamba's attribution
[1934 and 1936], dating it to
about 1470, with which Salvini
agrees.

24 ⊞ ◑ 120×65 *1469–70* 目 ⦂

**Madonna and Child in a
Glory of Seraphim** Florence,
Uffizi
Recorded in the inventories of
1784 as an anonymous work,
it was attributed to Botticelli by
Bode [1893], and accepted by
all except A. Venturi [1925]. It
is the first work in which one
can note that "unnatural"
longilineal sense of the figure
which was to be characteristic
of Botticelli. The panel is still in
its original frame. Some of the
glazing is gone, and the color,
particularly in the Virgin's
mantle, is worn. The gilding has

24

26 (plate II)

gone in part and much has
darkened. It is harmed, too, by
an unpleasant greenish varnish.

25 ⊞ ◑ 124×64 *1469–70* 目 ⦂

**Madonna and Child
(Madonna of the Rosebush)**
Florence, Uffizi
Transferred in the eighteenth
century from the Chamber of
Commerce, Florence, to the
Uffizi, where it was entered
in the inventory as a work by
Botticelli. Since Ulmann [1893],
critics acknowledge its
authenticity (with the sole
exception of Morelli [1897]),
dating it near *Fortitude* (26)
because of the way the paint is
applied. The panel was badly
varnished in the nineteenth
century.

26 ⊞ ◑ 167×87 1470 目 ⦂

Fortitude Florence, Uffizi
The first work of Botticelli
documented and mentioned in
ancient sources [Albertini,
1510, etc]. Painted for the
hall of the Arte della
Mercanzia then in Piazza della
Signoria at the corner of Via de'
Gondi; then on the ground
floor of the Uffizi Palace, when
it was recorded by Cinelli in
1677. With the suppression of
the guild (1777), it was put in
storage, and since 1861 it has
been exhibited at the Uffizi. A
series of paintings of the Seven
Virtues had been commissioned
of Piero del Pollaiuolo on 18
December 1469. In May 1470
1470 Tommaso Soderini, the
new consul of the guild,
commissioned Botticelli to
paint *Fortitude*. It was confirmed
by the guild on 18 June, and
payment in full was made on
18 August. A second Virtue, also
commissioned of Botticelli, was
never painted, perhaps because
of Pollaiuolo's protestations.
This may be the cause of the
plea presented in January 1471
by a group of painters to their
own guild *(Medici e Speziali)*
"that care be taken in future that
commissions once assigned to
one painter not subsequently be
assigned to others." In this
painting Botticelli shows in the
gilding, decoration, and
handling of metal that he was
well acquainted with work in
precious metals.

27 ⊞ ◑ 167×195 1470* 目 ⦂

**Sacra Conversazione (The
Convertite Altarpiece ?)**
Florence, Uffizi
Transferred from the Church of
Sant'Ambrogio to the

27

Accademia, and thence to the Uffizi in 1946. It depicts the Madonna enthroned between Saints Mary Magdalene, John the Baptist, Francis, Catherine of Alexandria, standing; Cosmas and Damian, kneeling, with the features of Lorenzo and Giuliano de' Medici. Since sixteenth-century sources mention among Botticelli's works a "panel in the Church of the Augustinian nuns of Santa Elisabetta delle Convertite," where the picture still was in 1802, some scholars have identified this as the panel in question, [Gamba, 1931, 1932 and 1936] without presenting conclusive evidence, because there is no surviving description of the Convertite panel and because the saints depicted are not the patrons of that convent. This doubt, accepted by Mesnil and supported by Yashiro [1929], who suggests that the Convertite panel is really the Lee *Trinity* (151), although this attribution seems less plausible. In any case, the present work is very close in time to *Fortitude*. Much repainting in the sixteenth century has changed the appearance of the Medicis as well as the Madonna and Child, who now seem Peruginesque. Perhaps the original appearance of the Madonna was similar to 28.

28 ⊞ ◑ 83,5×45,5 ▤ ⦂

Madonna and Child Enthroned Formerly Lockinge House (Wantage), Thomas Lloyd Collection
Removed about 1900 from the Graziani Chapel at Comezzano (Vaggio), it was sold by Giovanni Magherini Graziani in November 1903 to the Florentine antique dealer Elia Volpi, who sold it to Lady Wantage in 1904. It was in that collection until 1947. It was published in 1904–5 by the Arundel Club as an autograph work; Berenson [1924] and many others attributed it to the workshop. This seems correct, although it may have been executed under Botticelli's direct supervision (but apparently by the same hand that copied the Duveen *Madonna* [117]).

Probably a variant copy of the similar figures in the so-called Convertite Altarpiece (27) as it was before sixteenth-century repainting [Berenson, 1927].

29 ⊞ ◑ 50×141 1472* ▤ ⦂

The Adoration of the Magi London, National Gallery

28

In 1845 it passed from the Orlandini to the Lombardi-Baldi Collection, both in Florence, and to the National Gallery in 1875. There has been much controversy because of the many changes, retouchings and *pentimenti* that appeared in the 1940 restoration. The left side is much worked while the right side, which seems to have been painted later, is clear and direct. Among the group of worshipers are several heads that have been attributed to Filippo Lippi in the period he was influenced by Fra Angelico. More certainly by Botticelli are the kneeling kings, the figure immediately behind them looking at the star, his companion, the Madonna, St Joseph and the two shepherds (which reappear in later works), the dwarf and the figures around him. For the rest, Filippino Lippi would seem to be the painter. Thus two hypotheses are possible: 1) that the panel was laid out by Filippo Lippi and then given to Botticelli when he was in the workshop as an exercise (the same thing happened when Filippino joined Botticelli's workshop); 2) that the panel was laid out while Filippino was still in his father's workshop, continued when Filippino went to Botticelli's workshop, and then hastily finished by Botticelli himself. The work is believed to have been finished in 1472, or by 1475 at the latest, according to scholars since Horne [1908].

30 ⊞ ◑ 8,2×12,6 1471* ▤ ⦂

The Annunciation Glens Falls (New York), Louis F. Hyde Collection
Considered a youthful work by L. Venturi [1933] and most scholars, close to the presumed Convertite Altarpiece (27) of 1471. Van Marle dated it to 1490, but Salvini returned to the

29 (plates IV-VI)

30

earlier date because of elements of Verrocchio's style.

31 ⊞ ◑ 84×65 1471* ▤ ⦂

Madonna and Child with an Angel Bearing Grain and Grapes (Madonna of the Eucharist) Boston, Isabella Stewart Gardner Museum
Transferred from Palazzo Chigi, Rome, to Boston early in the twentieth century.
Unanimously considered autograph (since Morelli [1891], who confirmed the traditional attribution) and dated about 1471–2, except for Schmarsow [1923], who dates it after Botticelli's stay in Rome. Marvelous synthesis by Botticelli of elements of Verrocchio with those of Pollaiuolo. The painting is full of new meaningful allusions to the Eucharist – in contrast to the Lippian motif (with the bread and wine of the Mass suggested by the grain and bunches of grapes replacing the motif of the Child taking pieces of pomegranate). And there also seem to be neo-Platonic elements [Post, 1914].

There is a workshop copy in the Musée Condé, Chantilly, where there is a flowered backrest in place of the landscape and where the basket is full of roses. Another copy (82 × 42 cm.) is in the collection of R. Benson, London, with several changes in the architecture and the sky, and with a vase of flowers. A good old copy of the head of the Madonna is mentioned by Yashiro in his own collection.

32 ⊞ ◑ 65×41 1471* ▤ ⦂

Portrait of Esmeralda Bandinelli (?) London, Victoria and Albert Museum
Acquired from the Pourtalès Collection by Dante Gabriele Rossetti, who may have restored it, adding the apocryphal [Ulmann, etc.] legend *Smeralda di M. Bandinelli*

32

33

moglie di Vi. Bandinelli. Left to the Victoria and Albert by Jonides. The dating is controversial: 1470 [Schmarsow; Van Marle; Gamba], 1482 [Ulmann; Kroeber], but the influence of Verrocchio tempered by that of Pollaiuolo suggests 1471 as most probable

33 ⊞ ◑ 78×55,4 ▤ ⦂

Madonna and Child with two Angels Chicago, Art Institute (Ryerson Collection)
After many transfers, it went to the Martin A. Ryerson Collection from that of E. F. Weber, Hamburg. Berenson considers it an old copy. The catalogue of the museum attributes it to the school and dates it about 1475. The technique is correctly described as mixed (tempera and oil).

34 ⊞ ◑ *55×30* ▤ ⦂

Portrait of a Youth Formerly Zurich, Günther Abels Collection
Attributed to Botticelli by Bode [1926], no later than 1475. Agreed by Van Marle and ignored by other scholars.

35 ⊞ ◑ 89,5×44,4 ▤ ⦂

Portrait of a Young Man New York, Metropolitan Museum
It passed in 1912 from the Jean Dollfus Collection to the Rogers Foundation, which gave it to the museum in 1918. Attributed to Botticelli by Van Marle, who dated it 1470–2, and Berenson [1932]. More likely the work of a follower, near to Sellaio or

31

34

35

Raffaellino del Garbo, according to Salvini.

36 ⊞ ⊘ 81×53 1471* 目 ⋮

Portrait of a Lady with the Attributes of a Martyred Saint (Catherine ?) Altenburg, Staatliches Lindenau Museum

Those who accept its attribution to Botticelli (traditionally ascribed to Ghirlandaio) suggest 1471 [Van Marle; Gamba; Schmarsow; Kroeber] when Galeazzo Sforza visited Lorenzo the Magnificent in Florence. (On that visit Sforza was painted by Piero del Pollaiuolo, and Verrocchio depicted his wife, Bona of Savoy.) Thus, the lady would be Bona Sforza or another lady of the family. The date might be 1481, when Caterina Sforza married Girolamo Riario in Rome. The last seems more likely because of the similarity to the medallions and frescoes of her in Rome and Milan. But 1481 would not suit the attribution to Botticelli. And the composition is not like him; it lacks his sense of unity. But perhaps there were considerable retouching and changes made later. Among those who reject the attribution to Botticelli are A. Venturi (who ascribed it to Piero di Cosimo), Gottschewski [1908] and Mesnil, while Yashiro and Bettini do not mention the work.

37 ⊞ ⊘ diam. 131,5 1473* 目 ⋮

The Adoration of the Magi London, National Gallery

Vasari mentions this as being in the Pucci house [1568], where it was inventoried in 1698. It passed to the

Guicciardinis (1720) in the dowry of Luisa Ninfa de' Pucci, and thence through several English collections. It was probably a separate panel and thus to be seen at eye level. Thus the excessively tall buildings in the background would flatten out and the huge blocks in the foreground would stand out more, giving a greater sense of depth and more unity. It represents an anticipation of anamorphic distortion, particularly in respect of Leonardo, who is usually considered the first Western artist to use it. The young man in the foreground looking out may be a self-portrait of Botticelli [Konody, 1908]. In any case, other hands seem to have collaborated. Certain details suggest Filippino Lippi [Salvini]. The more likely datings vary between 1472 [Yashiro; A. Venturi; Van Marle; Gamba; Mesnil] and 1476 [Horne; Chastel]. In any case it seems earlier than the Uffizi *Adoration of the Magi* (50).

38 A ⊞ ⊘ 31×25* 1472-73 目 ⋮

The Finding of the Body of Holofernes Florence, Uffizi

This may have formed a diptych with the following painting, given (c 1580) by Rodolfo Sirigatti to Bianca Cappello, the wife of Francesco I, Grand-Duke of Tuscany [Borghini, 1584]. Her inheritance went to her son Antonio de' Medici, Prince of Capistrano, and on his death (1632) to the Uffizi. In the acute finesse of details and in the precise composition one can detect, in addition to the influence of Verrocchio and Pollaiuolo just after 1470, the *faire petit* of Mantegna and the preciosity of the Ferrarese painters [Salvini]. Most scholars date it about 1472, except Argan, who dates it to 1470 [1957], and Yashiro and Bettini, who date it about 1467.

38 B ⊞ ⊘ 31×24* 1472-73 目 ⋮

The Return of Judith Florence, Uffizi See 38A above

A faithful copy of an oval panel (30·5 × 22 cm.) it passed from the Bardini Collection, Florence, to the New Gallery, New York [Yashiro, 1925].

39 ⊞ ⊘ 195×75 1473* 目 ⋮

St Sebastian Berlin, Staatliche Museen

Acquired with the Solly

37 (plates VII-IX)

Collection in 1821. Ascribed to Pollaiuolo until Cavalcaselle [1864] attributed it to Botticelli and identified it as the painting described by the Anonimo Gaddiano as being in Sta Maria Maggiore, Florence, where it was hung on a pillar of the central nave on 20 January 1474. It was probably no longer there by the time of the

36

second edition of Vasari's *Vite* [1568] and certainly not there in 1677, for Cinelli does not mention it. Similar in composition to the *St Sebastian* that Andrea del Castagno had painted about 20 years earlier (New York, Metropolitan Museum). It is much more spiritual than Pollaiuolo's contemporary *St Sebastian* (London, National Gallery). One can already detect a

Botticelli of meditative and melancholic introspection. The poplar panel is slightly damaged around the edges, particularly on the right.

40 ⊞ ⊘ 1473-75* 目 ⋮

Madonna and Child with two Angels Paris, Louvre

Considered a copy of Sellaio of Botticelli [Berenson, 1932], but it seems rather to be a collaborative effect of Botticelli and Filippino Lippi [Gamba; Mesnil; Berti and Baldini, 1957], with the former responsible for most of the figures of the Madonna and Child.

Another version, with only one angel, went from the Campana Gallery to the Musée Longchamp, Marseilles, where it was entered (1861) as a work by Filippino Lippi. It was later attributed to the school of Botticelli by Reinach, Bode and Yashiro. On the back is an old tag with the writing "Uboldi."

41 ⊞ ⊘ 57,5×44 1474* 目 ⋮

Portrait of a Man with a Medal of Cosimo the Elder Florence, Uffizi

It went to the museum in the bequest of Cardinal Carlo de' Medici (1666). The attribution to Botticelli was almost unanimous, from Morelli and Frizzoni [1888], except for Bode [1921 and 1926]. There has been no satisfactory identification of the man who holds the posthumous medal of Cosimo the Elder (terracotta-like stucco set into the panel and gilded). He was first identified as a member of the family (Piero the Gouty, Piero di Lorenzo, Giovanni di Cosimo) or as Pico della Mirandola. Then it was suggested that he might be the creator of the medal (Michelozzo or Niccolò Fiorentino or Cristoforo Geremia). One may cautiously consider then an accounts entry in the Medici papers (Florence, State Archives)

according to which, in 1475, Antonio, Botticelli's brother, received payment for casting medals. In other documents Antonio is mentioned for gilding medals connected to copies of originals by Pisanello now in Russia [Mandel, 1955]. Thus one might advance the hypothesis that this is a portrait of Antonio Filipepi holding in his hands a medal that he had cast or gilded (in fact the cast struck into the painting was not very successful). Furthermore there are great similarities between this man and the presumed self-portrait of Botticelli in the Uffizi *Adoration*

39

40

38 A (plate X)

38 B (plate XI)

41 (plate III)

89

of the Magi (50). If this is Antonio, it would fit the generally accepted dating of the picture, before 1470 [Gamba] or 1477 [Yashiro]. Only Ulmann suggested 1492, believing the man to be Piero the Gouty.

42

42 ▦ ◕ 44×32 1474* ▤ ⚬

Portrait of a Member of the Medici family Formerly Florence, Galleria Corsini
The man holds the diamond ring, private emblem of the Medicis. Attributed to Botticelli by many [Morelli, 1873; Bode, 1893; Waetzold, 1908; A. Venturi, 1924 and 1925; Berenson, 1932], rejected (particularly in favor of Pollaiuolo, to whom it was traditionally ascribed, or his circle) by others [Ulmann, 1893; Horne, 1908; Kroeber, 1911; Van Marle; Mesnil], and reattributed by Salvini, who dates it about 1474.

43 ▦ ◕ 1474* ▤ ⚬

Assumption of the Virgin Formerly Pisa, Cathedral
From payments made in 1474 and a mention by Vasari, it appears that this work was begun in the Chapel of the Incoronata. Unfinished, it was destroyed in 1583.

44 ▦ ◕ 1475 ▤ ⚬

Pallas (or Minerva) Formerly Florence, Palazzo Medici
This was a standard painted for the joust in Florence in 1475 and listed in the inventory (1492) of possessions left by Lorenzo the Magnificent and described in an account of the joust found by Magliabechi, from which it appears that the subject was similar to the *Pallas* in inlay at Urbino (p. 116).

45 ▦ ◕ *55×37* 1475* ▤ ⚬

Portrait of Lorenzo the Magnificent Formerly Paris, Lazzaroni Collection
Until about 1895 it was in the possession of the Counts Isolani di Castelvecchio (Bologna), together with its companion *Portrait of Giuliano de' Medici* (46). Should be considered – after Yashiro [1925], Van Marle, Mesnil and Salvini – an autograph of about 1475, because of the subject and for reasons of style.

46 ▦ ◕ 54,5×36,5 1475* ▤ ⚬

Portrait of Giuliano de' Medici Milan, Crespi Collection
Formerly in the collection of the Counts Isolani di Castelvecchio (see 45), it went to the Kahn

Scheme for identification of "modern" characters depicted in painting 50.

50 (plates XIII-XV)

Collection, New York, in 1914, and then to the Thyssen Collection, Lugano; the Crespis acquired it in 1956. A fine work, but stylistic elements of Botticelli are unclear. The composition suggests that it made a pair with 45. Related to this are three other paintings of Giuliano, albeit reversed (47 and 48), on which scholars are divided. Inclined to accept this as an autograph – first identified by Fry [1914] and Logan Berenson [*id*] – are A. and L. Venturi, Valentiner [1926], Gamba, Mesnil, Berenson and Salvini. The three copies seem to date from 1478, painted for friends after the murder of Giuliano. It is not known why the copies were reversed. The

copies are discussed separately below because of their different histories and because they have conflicting claims to be the prototype.

47 ▦ ◕ 54×36 1478 ? ▤ ⚬

Portrait of Giuliano de' Medici Berlin, Staatliche Museen
This was in Palazzo Strozzi, Florence, where in 1864 Cavalcaselle catalogued it as a work of Botticelli; agreed by Bode and Van Marle. Now it is generally considered a reverse copy of 46 *(q.v.)* hurriedly prepared in the workshop with final work by Botticelli. Another version, simplified

(tempera on panel, 54 × 36 cm.) went to the Accademia Carrara, Bergamo, in the Morelli bequest. One hesitates to identify Botticelli's hand in this one because of the rigidity of design and the heavy arrangement of masses, even though Morelli, Ulmann, Berenson and Wittgens considered it autograph and the prototype of the series.

48 ▦ ◕ 76×52,6 ▤ ⚬

Portrait of Giuliano de' Medici Washington, National Gallery (Samuel H. Kress Bequest)
Kress acquired this painting from an Italian collection (1949). This seems the best and most sensibly organized copy of the portrait of Giuliano (see 46). Bettini [1942], Suida and Shapley [1956] consider it the archetype (of 46 as well) and believe it was executed during Giuliano's lifetime. But the bird on the dead branch [Friedmann, 1956] and the half-open door [Salvini], classic symbols of death, would challenge this view. Yet it is possible that Botticelli had a large hand in the work, which seems the best executed of the copies.

49 ▦ ◕ 61×40 1475* ▤ ⚬

Portrait of a Young Woman Florence, Pitti
None of the attempted identifications of the subject (Simonetta Vespucci, Clarice Orsini, Fioretta Gorini, etc.) are satisfactory. More likely, albeit

challenged, is the attribution to Botticelli and a dating to about 1475 (although Ulmann gives 1482; Bode, 1490; and Schmarsow, 1481). In favor of attribution are Cavalcaselle, Ulmann, Bode, Schmarsow, the two Venturis, Van Marle, Mesnil, Bettini, Ciaranfi Francini, Chastel and Salvini; against it are Milanesi [1879], Morelli, Berenson (first [1899] in favor of a "friend of Sandro," then [1932] of Ghirlandaio), Horne (ascribing it to the school) and Yashiro (imitation). The sleeve unnaturally covers the hand. The harmony of the composition was altered by a repainting that covered part of the wall that originally showed behind her back (from the lower part of her shoulder blades down) and limited the light zone to 9.5 cm. from the bottom up.
A variant copy is in the Staatliche Museen, Berlin, which Rouchès [1950] alone considers autograph. It is probably a workshop copy.

50 ▦ ◕ 111×134 1475* ▤ ⚬

The Adoration of the Magi Florence, Uffizi
Mentioned by Albertini [1510], "Billi" [1515–16] and the Anonimo Gaddiano [1542–8] and more amply described by Vasari. These sources (along with Borghini and Baldinucci) agree that it was in Sta Maria Novella over the altar of the commissioner, Giovanni di Zanobi del Lama, or Lami, an eminent figure in the guild of moneychangers and in close contact with the Medicis. The patronage of the altar was late

Derived from 49 (Berlin, Staatliche Museen). (Below) Variation of 47 (Bergamo, Accademia Carrara).

45

46

47

48

51

ceded to the Fedinis, then to the Spanish merchant Fabio Mandragoni, who refurbished the frame after a design by Vasari and sold the whole to Bernardo Vecchietti, who replaced it with an *Annunciation* by Santi di Tito. From the Villa at Poggio Imperiale, where the painting was transferred, it went to the Uffizi in 1796. Full of members of the Medici family and their circle, the beautiful panel has been of particular interest to scholars, especially in identifying the figures.

Notwithstanding the view of most scholars, it is likely that the commissioner was called Gaspare rather than Giovanni, because the scene depicts the homage of King Gaspar. The most commonly agreed identifications of the figures are as follows, the number referring to those in the plan opposite: (5) Cosimo the Elder; (6) Piero the Gouty; (7) Giovanni de' Medici; (8) Giuliano de' Medici; (9) the commissioner Lami indicating himself [according to Ulmann, it is Filippo Strozzi]; (10) perhaps Giovanni Argiropulo; (12) Botticelli; (11) perhaps Lorenzo Tornabuoni; (2) Lorenzo the Magnificent; (3) Politian; (4) Pico della Mirandola (but, according to Gamba, it is Lami, though others identify the commissioner as 1 or 2). As for dating, there are various hypotheses, from 1475 [Bode; Gamba], to 1476 [Van Marle] or thereabouts [Salvini], to 1477 [Horne; A. Venturi; Mesnil; Chastel], to 1478 [Ulmann; Schmarsow]. If the last is right, it would be related to the Pazzi Plot (26 April 1478). Yashiro and Bettini date it later. The painting was much damaged and extensively restored, especially the Virgin's mantle, St Joseph and King Gaspar. The work was executed in an important period of Botticelli's career. The elements of Pollaiuolo are completely assimilated, and Botticelli expresses himself in an altogether personal idiom:

tense, compact, yet still open to some easy relaxed effects. (See the trees and the little boat in Plate XV, where the detail is twice actual size, showing the restoration in the face and in the sky.) The latter quality was to disappear in the absolute unity that was inaugurated with *Primavera* (58)

51 *200 × 300* 1476*

The Nativity Florence, Church of Sta Maria Novella
According to Gamba (followed

53

by Mesnil, Bettini and Salvini), this picture originally adorned the Lami Chapel – and was completely round – whence it was removed to the inside of the entrance to the church and adapted to its present lunette shape and surrounded by a broad frieze of simple festoons. Notwithstanding the damage, one can distinguish characteristic elements of Botticelli, first noted by Berenson [1932], after the picture had been generally attributed to the Florentine school or Lippi. Dated between 1476 and 1477.

A fresco copy (150 × 250 cm.) went from the Böhler Gallery, Munich, to the Kress Collection, New York, which transferred it to the Columbia Museum of Arts. Mesnil's opinion seems correct, that it is a workshop painting with

slight contributions by Botticelli, most of it due to Filippino Lippi.

52 40,5 × 30,5 1477*

Portrait of a Young Man
Philadelphia, Museum of Art (Johnson Collection)
By Botticelli according to Bode [1910], and Berenson [1932], who had previously ascribed it to a "friend of Sandro," accepted by Perkins [1905], who suggests that it is of Giuliano de' Medici. Neither Kroeber [1911] nor Van Marle think it is even of the workshop. Salvini ascribes it to a follower. Perhaps it was painted by Mariano d'Antonio when he was in Botticelli's workshop.

53 51,5 × 35 1476*

Portrait of a Man Formerly Naples, Museo Filangieri

54

Destroyed in World War II. It had been in the Filangieri Castle at Sapio (Avellino). Considered autograph by Frizzoni [1889], Van Marle, Gamba, Bode, Bettini, Mesnil and Salvini; rejected by Berenson and A. Venturi [1925] It has the nervous Botticelli line of *The Adoration* (50) and might thus be dated to about 1476 [Salvini]. It is possible that the unknown man depicted (a Medici, according to Mesnil) was the commissioner of *The Madonna of the Sea* (see 56).

54 51 × 36 1477*

Portrait of a Young Man
Washington, National Gallery of Art (Mellon Bequest)
Passed from the Liechtenstein Gallery, Vienna, to the Stout Collection, Chicago, and thence to Mellon. First considered autograph [Bode; Ulmann, 1893; to Mesnil], then attributed to Filippino Lippi [Scharf, 1935; to Berti and Baldini, 1957]; reattributed to Botticelli by Salvini [1957 and 1958], because of stylistic elements common to other works by Botticelli in this period (e.g., 49 and 50). Dated to 1470–1 by Kroeber [1911]; 1478–80 by Schmarsow, L. Venturi and Mesnil; 1475–8 by Bode [1926]; c. 1476 by Van Marle. It must be borne in mind that although Filippino was already mature, he was still working in Botticelli's studio at this period. Perhaps

Filippino did the clothing, unless it was altered later.

55 54 × 40 1477*

Portrait of a Young Man
Paris, Louvre
Acquired in 1882 from the Pillet Collection, Paris, where it was considered a "portrait of Burchiello" by Filippino Lippi. Ascribed to Botticelli by Ulmann [1893] and dated 1470–8; immediately rejected [Berenson, 1899; to A. Venturi, 1925] in favor of the school. Considered autograph by Bode [1921], Schmarsow [1923], Yashiro and Mesnil, while Scharf [1935], along with Berti and Baldini [1957], ascribed it to Filippino Lippi. Gamba and Salvini suggested a collaboration of the two painters and dated it about 1478.

A copy (55 × 40·7 cm.) in the

55

National Gallery of Scotland, Edinburgh, is generally ascribed to the workshop, except for Bodkins [1933], who considers it autograph.

56 40,3 × 28,4 1477*

Madonna and Child (Madonna of the Sea)
Florence, Galleria dell'Accademia
It came from the monastery of Sta Felicita, Florence. It is a pleasant devotional work, laid out with ease and rapidity. After Ulmann's indication [1893] as a work similar to Botticelli, the picture was

considered autograph by Gamba and Salvini and a workshop painting by Procacci [1951]. Boeck [1954], Berti and Baldini [1957] attribute it to Filippino Lippi, although it seems at most that he only collaborated. It was probably

56

commissioned by the man in the Naples portrait (53), because both pictures have the same heraldic cryptographic ribbon bow. The panel, damaged and repainted, was restored in 1956.

57 diam. 135 1477*

Madonna and Child with eight Angels (Raczinsky Tondo) Berlin, Staatliche Museen
It arrived in Paris as part of the Napoleonic booty and was purchased in 1824 by Count Raczinsky for 2,500 francs. Vasari mentions a *tondo* with almost life-size angels in S. Francesco near Porta San Miniato, Florence (Church of San Salvatore al Monte). He also mentions a copy with eight angels, executed by a student as a joke. Since we know of no other **tondo** with eight angels by Botticelli, this may have been that one. The fine quality of the work (considered autograph by Cavalcaselle [1864], Bode [1888], Ulmann, Schmarsow, Gamba and Salvini) does not exclude the possibility of collaboration by the workshop (according to Horne, Yashiro, A. Venturi,

57

49 (plate XII)

52

58 (plates XVI – XXI)

of love and of the ball. But the Humanist meaning of the painting remains, in accord with many contemporary texts, as does the identification of Venus with *Humanitas*, which separates the senses and material love, on the right, from the spiritual values, on the left. The theme may have been suggested by a letter in which Ficino, in 1477, expressed the hope that the young Lorenzo would find in devotion to Venus-*Humanitas* an equilibrium of all his gifts, entrusting him to his friends Vespucci and Naldi. If that were so, Botticelli might have been commissioned by Vespucci. Together with *The Birth of Venus* (72) and perhaps *Pallas and the Centaur* (71), this picture may have formed a group similar to the friezes (then unknown) that adorn the walls of the famous Villa of the Mysteries in Pompeii.

59 ⊞ ◉ diam. 95 1480* 🗐 :

Madonna and Young St John Adoring Christ

Piacenza, Pinacoteca Civica
This picture came from the Bardi Castle [1860]. Considered autograph by Pollinari [1890], Ferrari [1903], Gamba, Mesnil and Chastel. Berenson and Salvini consider it a collaboration between Botticelli and his workshop about 1480–1. Bode and Van Marle ascribe it to the school. Spoiled by old restorations and additions. It

62

does not seem to have its original form and dimensions, but Pucci's idea [1955] that it is a detached fresco transferred to panel seems unlikely.

60 ⊞ ⊕ 152×112 1480* 🗐 :

St Augustine in his Cell
Florence, Church of Ognissanti
The saint is in a library after the humanist fashion, when books were stored flat and not spine outward. The open volume on the shelf behind St Augustine shows Pythagoras' theorems. Mentioned in the sources, beginning with Albertini [1510], as a work commissioned by a Vespucci, in competition with Ghirlandaio, who frescoed a *St Jerome* on the pillar facing this. In 1564 the two frescoes were transferred to the wall of the nave. The details are described by Borghini [1584]. The Vespucci crest is painted on the architrave. It is a vigorous work, and it may have been influenced, as Horne [1908] suggests, by Botticelli's observation of Andrea del Castagno's works.

The Frescoes of Villa Lemmi

These frescoes adorned a loggia in a villa that seems once to have belonged to the Tornabuonis and was acquired by the Lemmis in the Chiasso Macerelli (formerly outside the city, but now in the city limits of Florence). The frescoes were uncovered in 1873. The first two were detached and were acquired by the Louvre. The third, badly worn, was left. At first they were connected to the marriage of Lorenzo Tornabuoni to Giovanna degli Albizi (1486). But Thieme [1897] questioned the identification of the bride in 61 B, and it was soon discovered that the pictures predated the marriage. Mesnil noted that the presumed Giovanna was very different from other depictions and pointed out that the crest near her was not of the Albizi, while

Berenson, Van Marle, L. Venturi and Chastel), but the master's hand is evident throughout. Ulmann and Gamba date it to 1475; Salvini to about 1477; Bode to 1478–80. The painting, on poplar panel, was damaged, particularly the face of the Madonna, and almost completely repainted.

58 ⊞ ◉ 203×314 *1477-78* 🗐 :

Primavera Florence, Uffizi
It is mentioned in the sources (Anonimo Gaddiano, Vasari, Medici inventories, etc.). It was painted for the villa in Castello, acquired in 1477 by Lorenzo and Giovanni di Pierfrancesco de' Medici. On Lorenzo's death, it passed, with the villa, to Giovanni delle Bande Nere; then in 1526 to his son, Cosimo I. In 1815 it was transferred from Castello to the Uffizi, then to the Accademia, and again to the Uffizi in 1919. The meaning of the allegory is uncertain. Among the more probable hypotheses is Warburg's [1893], who sees in it the reign of Venus sung by ancient poets and by Politian. To the right Zephyr pursues Flora, who, once possessed, becomes the "hour" of Spring and scatters flowers on the world. Venus, in the center, is *Humanitas*, patroness of the Medicean Humanists. Then there are the Three Graces dancing and Mercury dissipating the clouds. Jacobsen [1897] sees in it a "mystery" relating to the death of Simonetta Vespucci, reached by death and reborn in Elysium. Gombrich [1945] suggests the Judgment of Paris

59

60 (plates XXIII–XXV)

at the moment Venus enters the scene, after Apuleius' description in *The Golden Ass*. This interpretation, however, was rejected by Ficino and other humanists, who considered Venus a symbol of material love. But for the Humanists of the Medici court Mercury represented good counsel and reason, and the Three Graces – see Alberti – were identified with liberality (*Castitas, Pulchritudo, Amor*). In Alberti himself we find the concept of Hesiod (*Theogonia*, which describes a painting by Pythagoras of Paros mentioned in Pausanias' *Attica*) and the interpretation of Seneca *(De beneficiis):* "Eglie, Heufrosines, Thalia, as they were painted, took each other by the hand, laughing, with their clothing loose and clean, by which was intended liberality, that which one of these sisters gives, another receives, and the third gives the benefice thereof." Botticelli seems, however, to have turned to the original of Hesiod rather than to Alberti, for there are many details described by the Greek author and omitted by Leon Battista Alberti. Another interpretation would agree with certain verses of Politian, according to which some of the characters would be identified with the months from February (Zephyr) to September (Mercury), bearing in mind that the ancients refrained from

naming or describing the four months of winter [Battisti, 1954]. More recently Welliver [1957] suggested that it was an exhortation to Giuliano de' Medici to try to win a cardinal's hat from Pope Sixtus IV. G. Arciniegas [*Come nacque la Primavera*, printed in *Conferenze dell'Associazione Culturale Italiana*, fascicle X, 1963] suggests that it merely depicts a ball at which Simonetta Vespucci appeared as Flora, on the right, and, on the left, as a Grace with Eleonora of Naples and Albiera of Florence, while Venus, after the description of Isidoro Del Lungo, is the queen

61 A

61 B

the real crest on the other side was only later added *a secco*. The young woman resembles instead the unidentified lady – perhaps a sister of Lorenzo Tornabuoni – following Giovanna degli Albizi in Ghirlandaio's frescoed *Visitation* in the choir of Sta Maria Novella, Florence. Gombrich [1945] does not believe that Villa Lemmi once belonged to the Tornabuonis, but thinks it was a villa acquired by Lorenzo di Pierfrancesco de' Medici when he married Semiramide di Giacomo Appiani. This would be corroborated by the style of the frescoes, predating the Tornabuoni-Albizi wedding and earlier than the Sistine frescoes (63). Salvini dates them about 1483.

61A ⊞ ⊕ 227×269 / 1480* ⊟ ⋮

Young Man before the Arts
Paris, Louvre
The presumed Lorenzo Tornabuoni (see above), accompanied by a young woman – perhaps Minerva – is before the arts of the Trivium and the Quadrivium, presided over by Rhetoric. Much of the lower part of the fresco is gone.

61B ⊞ ⊕ 212×284 / 1480* ⊟ ⋮

Venus offers Gifts to a Young Woman accompanied by Graces Paris, Louvre
As mentioned above, the young woman was erroneously identified as Giovanna degli Albizi. This fresco has also lost much.

61C ▨ ⊕ 1480* ? ⊟ ⋮

Landscape with an Old Person Florence, Villa Lemmi
The old figure in a red garment can barely be seen, so worn is the fresco.

62 ⊞ ⊕ 243×550 / 1481 ⊟ ⋮

The Annunciation Florence, Forte del Belvedere
Fifteenth-century documents discovered by Poggi [1915–16] indicate that Botticelli painted this, for ten florins, between April and May 1481, to decorate (in the loggia of the Hospital of S. Martino alla Scala, Florence) the wall by the tomb of Cione Pollini, the founder of the hospice. When the hospice became the monastery of S. Martino alle Panche [1531], the loggia was transformed [1624] into the atrium of the church, and a double vault cut the fresco into two lunettes. In 1920 the fresco was detached, and in 1952 it was restored. Cavalcaselle attributed it to Filippino Lippi [1866]. After Horne [1908; but dating the work to c. 1490] generally attributed to Botticelli. The perspective is noteworthy: the foreshortening of the door and wall mark a sharp division between the room in which the Virgin is praying and the garden in which the Archangel appears. There are traces of the old gilding, though somewhat darkened.

The Frescoes in the Sistine Chapel

In the brief period in which relations were improved between Pope Sixtus IV della Rovere and Medici Florence, and perhaps at the suggestion of the Florentine architect Giovannino de' Dolci, the commissioner of Vatican building and the presumed builder of the Sistine Chapel, several artists – Cosimo Rosselli, Sandro Botticelli, Domenico Ghirlandaio and Perugino – were summoned from Florence to decorate the Sistine Chapel. Since Botticelli had finished the S. Martino fresco (62) in May 1481 and was again in Florence by 5 October 1482, where he accepted in person a commission for Palazzo della Signoria, his Roman sojourn must fall between these two dates. By a contract with Dolci dated 27 October 1481 (Secret Vatican Archives) the painters guaranteed to decorate the chapel with their assistants by 15 March 1482 at a price to be agreed on, depending on the judgment of samples to be submitted. On 27 January 1482 the price was established as 250 ducats per person. As a result either of the decision to increase the number of paintings or the wish to hasten the work, Signorelli and others were also commissioned. Vasari seems unreliable in stating that Botticelli directed the work, because Perugino had long since begun the fresco over the altar. In any case the various elements of the cycle seem to have been coordinated within a framework whose conception many critics attribute to Botticelli. This framework is in harmony with the ideas of Alberti, on which Botticelli often drew. (A partial plan of the whole is reproduced here. The ceiling, which was later to be frescoed by Michelangelo, was painted to resemble a starry sky by Piermatteo d'Amelia, probably in 1481.) Aside from the stories in the middle register of the walls (and the mock draperies painted below them), the cycle comprised 28 figures

martyred popes, depicted in pairs within the arch of each window. (They were originally depicted also on the altar wall, but were destroyed to make room for Michelangelo's *Last Judgment*.) They were identified by titles (according to tradition, dictated by Platina) written at their feet and concerning nationality, length of papacy and date of martyrdom. The scenes and the figures of popes were all frescoed, probably after *sinopie* [Camesasca, 1965], though the final touches were made *a secco*, and succeeded in covering the edges between each day's painting. Subsequent repainting in oil further masked the divisions. The final touches also included highlighting in gold. In the figures of the pontifs, lozenge inserts gave relief to their gems, robes, books, etc. (Most of these have fallen away as their holes show.) There was much help from assistants in the actual painting, though in Botticelli's case there were fewer than in the work of Perugino and others. Assistants probably painted the mock draperies below the painted scenes.

Catalogued below, together with the three scenes that sources credit to Botticelli, are those figures of Popes most authoritatively attributed to him [Cavalcaselle; Ulmann; Schmarsow; Berenson; Salvini; Camesasca] or to his school (assuming the ideas to have been provided by Botticelli). The dimensions mentioned refer to the height of the figure and the width (inside, bottom) of the niche within which it is depicted.

Scenes on the Wall

63A ▨ ⊕ 348.5×558 / 1481-82 ⊟ ⋮

The Life of Moses
In accord with the "parallelism" that regulates all the scenes on the walls of the Sistine Chapel, this fresco parallels *The Life of Christ*. The

following episodes are depicted (numbers referring to the illustration below): Moses (6), still unaware that he is a Jew, slays an Egyptian who had mistreated an Israelite, who (8) is then helped by a woman; Moses flees (7) to the land of Midian, where he puts to flight (5) the shepherds who had prevented Jethro's daughters from watering their flock; he helps the girls (4) and, having been employed by Jethro, removes his sandals (2) to enter the burning bush (1). Having faced this test, Moses (3) returns to Egypt with his family. This last episode is interpreted by Steinmann, Bode, Gamba and Mesnil as the Exodus, even though that would not fit the general sequence of the other episodes.

63B ▨ ⊕ 345.5×555 / 1481-82 ⊟ ⋮

The Life of Christ
This is also referred to as *The Purification of the Leper* after the principal episode. In the background are the

temptations (numbers referring to the illustration below): The devil in Franciscan habit – not to deride Sixtus IV's order, as some have suggested, but to show his subtle astuteness – asks (1) Christ to turn the stones to bread; then (2) asks Christ to leap from the Temple of Jerusalem; when Christ refuses the dominion of the world the devil leaps (3), while angels bring food. Having faced these tests, Christ returns to Galilee (4). Another interpretation is that he witnesses the purification of the leper he has healed. The scene in the foreground concerns the purification rite according to Deuteronomy 14:27. Among the many personages depicted, largely from life, the following have been tentatively identified: (9) Gerolamo Riario, the pope's nephew (though Schmarsow identifies him as a Della Rovere, master of the palace); (8) Giuliano della Rovere, later Pope Julius II (Gamba believes it is Raffaello Riario); (7) a Della Rovere, general of the Confraternity of Sto Spirito (Gamba thinks it is Ferrante

63 A (plates XXX-XXXI)

63 B (plate XXXII)

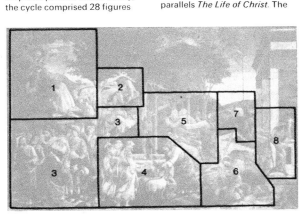

Scheme for identification of the episodes and Biblical characters depicted in painting 63 A.

Scheme for identification of Biblical and "modern" characters depicted in painting 63 B.

63 D   63 E   63 F   63 G   63 H   63 I

of Aragon, King of Naples); (5) Botticelli; (6) Filippino Lippi. According to Horne [1908], and his hypothesis is generally accepted, the scene illustrates Matthew 8: 4, and this would tie the scene more closely to the New Testament. It is possible that there was also intended a celebration of Pope Sixtus in the central building, the Hospital of Sto Spirito, which the Pope had built just at the time the fresco was painted. The two large oak trees allude to the pope's family name and have a heraldic function [Steinmann, 1905]. Less acceptable are two symbolic interpretations advanced by Schmarsow: that there is a parallel between the

sacrifice for the leper and Christ's future sacrifice; and a reference to the purification of the Florentines, under papal interdiction for having hanged the Archbishop of Pisa after the Pazzi Plot. The execution of the fresco seems almost entirely by Botticelli.

63C 348,5 × 570 / 1481 - 82

The Punishment of the Rebels
This is symbolically related to *The Giving of the Keys* frescoed on the opposite wall by Perugino. Korah, Dathan and Abiram, with their followers, refused to acknowledge the authority of Aaron and rebelled. In confrontation,

63 C (plates XXXIII-XXXIV)

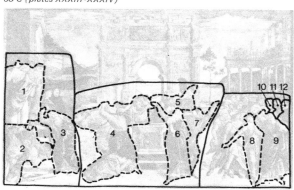

Scheme for identification of Biblical and "modern" characters depicted in painting 63 C.

divine election favored Aaron, and Moses punished the rebels. The numbers in the illustration below refer to: on the right, the rebels with stones in their hands held back by Achariot (8), while Moses (9) speaks; in the center, the trial by incense: at Moses' (6) request the priests perform the rite. The smoke from the thuribles of Aaron (5) and the faithful Eleazar (7) rise to heaven, while that of the rebels flames out at them and they fall to the ground (4). On the left, Moses (3) drives the rebels into the ground (2) while Aaron's two sons, Eldad and Medad (1) are miraculously raised up. The Renaissance building in the background on the left may be the synagogue. In the center is the Arch of Constantine in Rome bearing the epigraph NEMO SIBI ASSUMM/AT HONOREM NISI VOCATUS A DEO/TANQVAM ARON. The classical building on the right has been identified as the Septizonium as it must still have been at the time of Sixtus IV. Since Steinmann, aside from the meaning that accords with the general idea of the cycle, an allusion has been suggested to the absolute authority of Pope Sixtus IV, challenged at the time by Andreas Zamometič, Archbishop of Kraijn. Zamometič had, in the spring of 1481, openly spoken ill of the Pope and the Roman Curia and subsequently tried to organize a council to depose Sixtus IV, whom he referred to as the "Devil's son." Zamometič was arrested in June 1481 and stripped of the title of imperial legate. He was released from prison two months later and sent back to Germany, where he resumed his attack on Rome, secretly supported by Emperor Frederick III. Supporting this allusion is the inscription on the Arch of Constantine and the favorite hat of Sixtus IV worn by Aaron in the painting. Some of the witnesses in the painting, certainly taken from life, have been tentatively identified:

Drawing (118 × 196 mm.; Florence, Uffizi). The composition is similar to 63 C, variously considered preparatory by Botticelli or a derivation by Filippino Lippi.

(11) Botticelli, according to Steinmann and Gamba, though not by others; (12) Pomponio Leto (Cardinal Giorgio Costa for Schmarsow; Chierigati for Gamba); (10) Alessandro Farnese, later Pope Paul II, according to Steinmann and most critics (but Raffaello Riario for Schmarsow). Assistants seem to have had a larger hand here than in the preceding painting, and they may be responsible for the architectural features on the right.

The Popes

63D 210 × 85 / 1481 - 82

St Marcellinus
The inscription is S. MARCELLINVS. ROMANVS, the 29th pope. The work of Ghirlandaio's workshop, according to Ulmann. More likely it is by Botticelli's workshop, with Botticelli painting the face. The lower part of the figure was much damaged and repainted.

63E *210 × 90* / 1481 - 82

St Marcellus I
The inscription is S. MARCELLVS. ROMANVS, the 30th pope. It can be attributed to Botticelli's workshop, with the face by Botticelli. Much repainted.

63F *210 × 80* / 1481 - 82

St Sixtus II
The inscription is S. SIXTVS. SECVNDVS. GRECVS, the 24th pope, perhaps an Athenian. One of the most beautiful of the series, with Botticelli's hand much in evidence. Repainted from the waist down.

63G *210 × 80* / 1481 - 82

St Stephen I
The inscription is S. STEPHANVS. ROMANVS, the 23rd pope. It is one of the surest attributions to Botticelli. The lower part is much restored.

63H *210 × 80* / 1481 - 82

St Lucius I (?)
The inscription seems to read S. VOIVS ROMANVS, and some scholars have considered it that of a non-existent Pope Voius. Kraus [1902] advanced the hypothesis of St Lucius (because of the chronological arrangement of the figures). Modern scholars ascribe it to Botticelli albeit with reservations about the execution. Only the head is unaltered. The rest was damaged and repainted.

94

63 K   63 L   63 M   63 N

the face must be comparatively recent, judging from photographs taken about 50 years ago.

64 ⊞ ⊕ 47×35,5 1481-82 ▤ ⫶

St Thomas Aquinas Zurich, Abegg Stockar Collection
Many books reproduce the figure reversed; in fact, the figure looks to the left. It is possible that the saint's face is taken from that of Pope Sixtus IV. The vigorous characterization shows that Botticelli painted someone from the life. The painting came from the Holford Collection, Westonbirt (Gloucestershire). Ascribed to Botticelli by A. Venturi [1922], accepted by Berenson [1932], Gamba, Mesnil, Bettini, and Salvini. Dated 1481–2 by Venturi and Salvini, and to 1495 by Mesnil. Other scholars attribute the work to Tura [Phillips], Baldassarre Estense [Cook], Montagna, Gentile Bellini [Fry], Borsignori and Signorelli. Canvas applied to panel.

65 ⊞ ⊕ 48×35,5 1481-82 ▤ ⫶

Portrait of a Woman
London, Rothermere Collection
Formerly in the Trivulzio Collection, Milan. Considered autograph by Berenson [1936], L. Venturi [in Konody, 1932], Van Marle, Gamba and Salvini. Salvini dates it near the Sistine frescoes; L. Venturi dates it to 1475–6; and Gamba to c. 1478. A. Venturi [1925] and Mesnil reject the attribution. Much restored.

66 ⊞ ⊕ 44,5×29 1481-82 ▤ ⫶

The Redeemer Blessing
Detroit, Institute of Arts
From the Gavet Collection, Paris, it went to the Belmont Collection, Newport, and then to Valentiner, Detroit. Probably autograph [Yashiro; Van Marle; Berenson; Salvini] and probably the original of many copies and imitations (see 136) painted by the workshop [Mesnil]. It is possible that Botticelli himself imitated a lost *Christ Blessing* by Antonello, which was highly prized by Sixtus IV and was probably painted in Rome in 1450 [Mandel, 1956]. This would fit Van Marle's dating to to 1481–2, accepted by Salvini. Yashiro dates it to 1483–4.

Detail of right wall of Sistine Chapel, with 63 B and 63 M (above the former, left); below scene of The Life of Christ, *the mock drapery presumably painted by Botticelli's assistants, who were also responsible for the execution of some decorative elements (semi-pillars, cornices, window embrasures, etc.).*

63 I ⊞ ⊕ *215×80* 1481-82 ▤ ⫶

St Cornelius
The inscription is S. CORNELIVS. ROMANVS, the 21st pope. It is much repainted but characteristic elements of Botticelli survive in the face.

63 J ⊞ ⊕ *210×85* 1481-82 ▤ ⫶

St Callistus I
The inscription reads S. CALISTVS. ROMANVS, the 17th pope. Executed entirely by the workshop in all likelihood. Much damaged.

63 K ⊞ ⊕ *210×80* 1481-82 ▤ ⫶

St Soter
The inscription is S. SOTHER. ITALVS. EX. FVNDIS, the 13th pope, perhaps a native of Fondi. The idea was probably Botticelli's, but the execution was by the workshop. Much damaged.

63 L ⊞ ⊕ *210×80* 1481-92 ▤ ⫶

St Anicetus
The inscription is S. ANICETVS. SIRVS, the 12th pope, perhaps from Emesa. Although damages do not impede ascription of the idea to Botticelli, they preclude judgment of the execution.

63 M ⊞ ⊕ *220×80* 1481-92 ▤ ⫶

St Telesphorus
The inscription is THELESPHORVS. GRECVS, the 8th pope, perhaps from Turio in Magna Grecia. The composition is Botticelli's, but the work is so damaged that one cannot say more.

63 N ⊞ ⊕ *210×80* 1481-82 ▤ ⫶

St Evaristus
The inscription is S. EVARISTVS. GRECVS, the 6th pope. Notwithstanding much damage one can still detect the hand of Botticelli. Damage to

Detail of 63 N from an early twentieth-century photograph: comparing it with the whole reproduced above from a recent photograph one notices serious deterioration and almost total disappearance of facial features.

64

65

66

95

67 ⊞ ⊘ 70,2 × 104,2 1481 - 82* ▤ ⋮

The Adoration of the Magi
Washington, National Gallery
(Mellon Bequest)
Weak attempts have been
made to identify some of the
figures as nephews of Pope
Sixtus IV. Acquired in Rome by
the French engraver Perallis,
who sold it to the Hermitage,
Leningrad, as a work of
Mantegna. Waagen [1864]
recognized it as a Botticelli. Put
up for sale in 1933, it entered
the Mellon Collection (1940).
It may be the *Adoration* that
the Anonimo Gaddiano says was
painted in Rome. Confirming
this would be the angular oaks,
the heraldic emblem of the
Della Roveres, along with
similarities to the manners of
Perugino and Signorelli, with

1927], L. Venturi [1926], Van
Marle and Gabrielli. But most
follow Cavalcaselle in ascribing
it to the workshop, albeit
conceding [Salvini] that
Botticelli had a hand in it,
shown by the freshness of line
and the sensitive handling of
paint. In any case, it must be a
copy of a classical marble:
either the *Venus* recorded by
Benvenuto Rambaldi as
among the Medici possessions
since 1375 or a work seen in
Rome. Following this
hypothesis, it seems that this
figure served Botticelli for his
Pallas and the Centaur and for
The Birth of Venus (71 and 72).
A copy (148 × 62 cm.),
generally considered workshop
(autograph only for A. Venturi
[1925]), like the original passed
from Palazzo Ferroni to the

came from the Solly Collection.
Considered autograph and the
prototype of similar Venuses by
Bode [1888, 1921 and 1926]
and Schmarsow [1923];
Ulmann considers it a reworking
by the master; and the others
ascribe it to the workshop.

70 ⊞ ⊘ 192 × 105 ▤ ⋮

Pomona or Autumn
Chantilly, Musée Condé
From Rome it passed to the
French Reiset Collection,
where Cavalcaselle saw it; he
was the first to ascribe it to
Botticelli [1864]. Earlier
Selvatico had attributed it to
Mantegna. A. Venturi [1911],
Bode [1926], Gamba, Mesnil
and Salvini ascribe it to the
workshop. It has iconographic
similarities to the drawing by

Botticelli of *Abundance*
(London, British Museum)
and with the woman carrying
firewood in *The Life of Moses*
(63 A). But this picture may be
a posthumous copy. There was
a copy in the collection of the
Marquis of Chennevière in
Alençon. There are two similar
copies in the Rosebery
Collection, London.

71 ⊞ ⊘ 207 × 148 1482* ▤ ⋮

**Pallas and the Centaur
(Minerva and the Centaur)**
Florence, Uffizi
Once the property of Lorenzo
and Giovanni di Pierfrancesco
de' Medici, according to an
inventory of 1516, it was
inherited by Giovanni delle
Bande Nere and was still in the
villa at Castello in 1598 and
1638, according to the
inventories; it went to the Pitti
about 1830; then to the royal
apartments (1856); and finally
to the Uffizi, after 1893. As for
the interpretation, scholars are
divided between political and
moral allegory. In the former
case, according to E. Ridolfi
[1893], the theme is related to
the diplomatic skill of Lorenzo
the Magnificent when in
1480 he persuaded the King of
Naples to abandon Sixtus IV's
league against Florence. Thus,
the background would depict
the city and bay of Naples; the
centaur would symbolize
Rome; and Pallas, holding the
Florentine halberd, would
represent Florence. For Horne,
the political allegory refers to
the alliance of Lorenzo with
Innocent VIII (1487). The
moral allegory — according to
Wittkower [1939] and
Gombrich [1945] and
accepted by Salvini and the
present writer — would relate to
Ficino's saying: *Bestia noster*
[*sic*], *id est sensus; homo
noster, id est ratio*, which
would describe the centaur
(explaining its double nature,
bestial and human, the latter
led by Minerva-Reason). This
might be interpreted, then, as an
appeal to Lorenzo di Pierfrancesco to let himself be
guided by Lorenzo the
Magnificent, whose personal
emblem adorns Pallas' dress.
Dating varies according to the
interpretation of the subject:
c. 1480 [Ridolfi; Berenson,
1895; Yashiro], c. 1488 [Horne;
L. Venturi, 1937], c. 1485 [Bode,
1921; Mesnil; Bettini], 1482-3
[A. Venturi, 1925; Van Marle;
Gamba], c. 1482 according to
Salvini, referring to similarities —
in the centaur — to a Vatican
sarcophagus [Tietze Conrat,
1925] and — in the breadth of the
landscape — to similarities to
Perugino and Signorelli, with
whom Botticelli worked in the
Sistine Chapel. Restored in
1953.

72 ⊞ ⊘ 172,5 × 278,5 1482* ▤ ⋮

The Birth of Venus Florence,
Uffizi
Together with *Primavera* and
Pallas and the Centaur (58 and
71), this belonged to Lorenzo
and Giovanni di Pierfrancesco
de' Medici. Housed in the villa
at Castello, it had the same
history as *Primavera*, passing

67 (plates XXVIII–XXIX)

whom Botticelli worked in the
Sistine Chapel. Bode and
Schmarsow, however, date it
between 1473 and 1475;
Van Marle to 1484. The
unusually emphasized
chiaroscuro led Mesnil to
think that Botticelli had in
mind the *Adoration* that
Leonardo painted in Florence
in 1481.
A copy on canvas, in the
Uffizi reserve, was published by
the *Burlington Magazine*
[1903] and by Reinach.

68 ⊞ ⊘ 162 × 74 ▤ ⋮

St Sebastian at the Column
Rome, Pinacoteca Vaticana
From the warehouses of
Castelgandolfo (1923).
Considered autograph by
A. Venturi [1924 and 1925] and
near in time to the *Pietàs* of
Munich and Milan (see 134 and
135). More justifiably assigned
to an imitator by Van Marle,
Gamba and Salvini, and
datable, according to the
present author, to the Roman
period. Damaged; restored in
1924.

69 ⊞ ⊘ 174 × 77 1482* ▤ ⋮

Venus Turin, Galleria
Sabauda
In 1844 it passed from
Palazzo Ferroni, Florence, to
the Davenport Bromley
Collection, London; in 1863
to the Ashburton at Bath House;
then to the Gualino, Turin, from
1920 to 1930; then to the
Italian Embassy in London,
until 1940. Considered
autograph, after Waagen
[1854] by A. Venturi [1925 and

69

Davenport Bromley Collection,
then to the Ashburton
Collection (1863), and then to
the Böhler Gallery, Munich,
which sold it to a collector in
Lucerne, whence it returned to
the market. Another copy
(157 × 68 cm.) is in the
Staatliche Museen, Berlin, and

68

*Copies of 69 (formerly Lucerne
and Berlin). (Below) Drawing
(317 × 253 mm.; London,
British Museum), universally
attributed to Botticelli and
related to painting 70.*

71 (plate XXXV)

70

72 (plates XLIV-XLV)
from the grand-ducal wardrobe in 1815 to the Uffizi. The subject comes from [J. Meyer, 1890] Homer and Latin literature, specifically from Ovid (*Metamorphoses*, II, 27; *Fasti*, V, 217), who describes the Hour handing a cloak to Venus Anadyomene, and from later Humanist literature. Others consider it the arrival of Venus, propelled by Zephyr and Chloris, in Sicily (after the anonymous poem *Pervigilium Veneris*, of the 2nd–3rd century) or in Portovenere, where Simonetta Vespucci lived [Schmarsow, 1923]. More likely is a neo-Platonic interpretation, advanced by Argan [1956] and, perhaps better, by Gombrich [1945], of the scene as the birth of *Humanitas*, created by Nature with its four elements and the union of spirit and matter. In Politian's *Stanzas*, the description of the birth of Venus does not so much suggest the subject of this painting as literally describe it. The technical details of execution seem very near those of *Pallas and the Centaur*. An analysis of the composition suggests that perhaps 30 or 35 cm. have been removed from the top of the picture. Thus *Primavera*, painted just before the departure for Rome, *Pallas* and this painting were housed together and had the same height. And the last two would have been painted just after Botticelli's return to Florence from Rome, to complete a single commission. The most common datings are c. 1478

74 A

74 B

74 C

74 D

[Bode] and 1485–6 [Schmarsow; to Argan], though Yashiro [1929] suggests 1487. Relating it to the Roman period was suggested by Van Marle, and Salvini went on to specify 1482.

73 ⊞ ◉ 54,5 × 47,4 / 1481-83 ? ▤ ⦂
Dante Alighieri Cologny (Switzerland), Martin Bodmer Collection
The frame, usually omitted from reproductions (perhaps because it was believed to be of wood) is painted and forms a whole with the portrait. The possession of Lord Charles Seymour, London, until 1892, it then went to the Langton Douglas Collection and (c. 1930) to the Burns of Hatfied, who sold it in 1947. Considered autograph by all except Kroeber [1911] and Mesnil. The dating is controversial: for Berenson and Gamba it is close to *The Birth of Venus* (72); for Ferri and Bertini, about 1495; but most relate it to the late drawings for *The Divine Comedy* (1498). The absence of certain data suggests a cautious ascription to 1481–3, the period in which most of Botticelli's rare canvases were painted.

Numerous restorations have partially altered the original composition.

The Story of Nastagio degli Onesti

The series of four scenes may have been commissioned by Lorenzo the Magnificent for the wedding of Giannozzo Pucci and Lucrezia Bini, which took place in 1483 [Horne] (see also 74 C.). In the possession of the Puccis until 1868, the paintings were sold for 100,000 lire to Barker of London [Milanesi, 1879]; briefly in the Leyland Collection; acquired in 1892 by

Aynard, Lyons, who soon sold the first three to the Spiridon Collection, Paris, whence they passed to the Cambó Collection, Barcelona, and then to the Prado, Madrid. The fourth went to the Donaldson Collection and then to the Watney, Charlbury. Laid out by Botticelli, they were largely executed by the workshop (though in varying degrees), in particular, by Jacopo del Sellaio and Bartolomeo di Giovanni [Richter, *Kunstchronik* XV; to Salvini]; but J. A. Gaya Nuño [Prado Catalogue, 1958] considers them largely autograph. The subject comes from Boccaccio [*Decameron*, V, 8].

74 A ⊞ ◉ 83 × 138 / 1483 ▤ ⦂
First Episode Madrid, Prado
Nastagio degli Onesti, who retired to the pine forest of Ravenna after being rejected by the daughter of Paolo Traversari (left background), wanders deep in thought (left foreground). A lady appears pursued by a knight and his dogs. They bite her as Nastagio tries to help her (center and right) There is a free copy, perhaps by Bartolomeo di Giovanni, in the Johnson Collection, Philadelphia.

74 B ⊞ ◉ 82 × 138 / 1483 ▤ ⦂
Second Episode Madrid, Prado
In the foreground, Nastagio is horrified to see the Knight tear out the lady's heart and give it to the dogs. Then the lady revives and the chase continues (center background). The knight meanwhile explains to Nastagio that he is Guido, his ancestor, who was rejected by his beloved and committed suicide. Divine justice has punished them both, and they must continue their chase one year for every month that the lady tormented Guido.

74 c ⊞ ◉ 84 × 142 / 1483 ▤ ⦂
Third Episode Madrid, Prado
Nastagio invites the Traversaris with their daughter to a banquet at the place where he had the vision. When the knight and the lady reappear, Nastagio explains the story. Then Paolo Traversari's daugher accepts Nastagio's suit (extreme right). The hand of Bartolomeo di Giovanni is more evident in this scene. On the pines to the left, the Pucci crest, in the center the Medici crest, to the right the two joined, which indicates the marriage of a Pucci man with a Bini woman. This refutes the commentators on Vasari [1846] who suggested a relation to the marriage of Pierfrancesco Bini with Lucrezia Pucci, in 1487. It confirms the hypothesis of Horne mentioned above.

74 D ⊞ ◉ 83 × 142 / 1483 ▤ ⦂
Fourth Episode Charlbury, Watney Collection
The wedding banquet of Nastagio degli Onesti and Paolo Traversari's daughter. Above the front capitals are the crests of the Puccis, the Medicis, and the two joined with laurels, the symbol of Lorenzo, the groom's uncle. From the second crest hangs a diamond-point ring, the private emblem of the Medicis. The guests use forks, rare in Europe at that time. In this panel and that preceding there are echoes of *The Feast of Herod*, painted by Filippo Lippi in Prato, perhaps with the assistance of Botticelli. Much work, too, by Jacopo del Sellaio in this panel.

75 ⊞ ◉ 69 × 173,5 / 1483* ▤ ⦂
Venus and Mars London, National Gallery
Acquired in Florence by Sir Alexander Barker (c. 1865), it went to London in 1874. It may have been done for the Vespuccis, for some wasps (It. *vespe*) are coming out of a trunk on the right [Gombrich, 1945]. Probably a backrest,

73

75 (plates XXXVI-XXXVII)

like similar subjects painted by Jacopo del Sellaio, Piero di Cosimo, and others. There may also be some neo-Platonic meanings: Venus-*Humanitas* has a beneficient power over Mars, god of discord and war [Robb, *Neoplatonism in the Italian Renaissance*; Gombrich]. Venus as love and concord is opposed to Mars, symbol of hate and discord. She conquers him by reason of the harmony of opposites, according to Ficino and Pico della Mirandola [Wind, 1950]. Also mentioned as literary sources are Lucretius, Politian (*Stanzas for the Joust*), Lorenzo the Magnificent (*Hymn to Mars and Venus*) [Palm, 1944], Reposiano (*De concubitu Martis et*

76

77 (plate XXXIX)

80

Veneris, 3rd cent.) [Wickhoff, 1906]. Bode [1921 and 1926], in accord with Van Marle, dated it to 1476–8; Schmarsow and Argan to 1475; Horne, Yashiro, both Venturis, Gamba, Mesnil, Bettini and Davies all tend to the period between 1485 and 1486; yet

the most probable dating is Salvini's, c 1483. In 1943 old repainting was removed.

76 ⊞ ◓ 82×54 / 1480-85 ▤ ⁝
Portrait of a Young Woman
Frankfurt, Städelsches Kunstinstitut
The lady wears around her neck a gem depicting Apollo and Marsyas, that belonged to the Medicis in the fifteenth century. Warburg [1892] – who recognized the picture as Botticelli's – identified the subject as Simonetta Vespucci. Van Marle agreed because of the similarity to the well-known portrait of the lady by Piero di Cosimo in Chantilly. Accepting the ascription to Botticelli are Ulmann and Van Marle; Bode [1926] with reservations; according to other recent scholars a workshop painting, albeit well done. It is possible that Botticelli laid it out and helped with the actual painting, which is due chiefly to Jacopo del Sellaio. Dating varies between 1478 [Bode], 1485 [Gamba] and c. 1490 [A. Venturi, 1925].

77 ⊞ ◓ 37,5×28,2 / 1483* ▤ ⁝
Portrait of a Young Man
London, National Gallery
Perhaps in the Udny Collection until 1804, and attributed then to Giorgione; then in the Northwick Collection – where Waagen first ascribed it [1837] to Filippino and then [1854] to Masaccio – and then to its present location in 1859. Cavalcaselle reascribed it to Botticelli [1864], followed by Richter [1883], Frizzoni [1891], Horne, Berenson and most modern scholars (except Ulmann and Bode), dating it to 1483–4 (except Gamba, who suggested 1490).

78A ⊞ ◓ 59×40 ▤ ⁝
Portrait of a Young Woman
London, National Gallery
From the Barker Collection, London, where it was considered autograph, it passed to the Samuel in 1874; then to the Cohen Collection, whence it returned to the Samuel, which gave it to the museum in 1906. On the back is an *Angel* (78B), ascribed to the workshop by Kroeber [1911], who yet considered the portrait autograph. For Mesnil the lady is from the workshop, and generally – after Davies [1951] – it is considered to be by a "pedestrian follower."

78B ⊞ ◓ 59×40 ▤ ⁝
Angel London, National Gallery
Painted on the back of the preceding. It may depict Goodness who finally prevails over the world and is raised to heaven. Because of its "general Botticellianism," Salvini considered it of the workshop. Nevertheless this attribution is generally rejected or ignored by modern scholars.

79 ⊞ ◓ 1483* ▤ ○
Mythological Scenes (?)
Formerly Volterra, Villa dello Spedaletto

Part of a cycle mentioned in a letter from an agent to Ludovico il Moro about 1485 (see *Outline Biography*, 1483).

80 ⊞ ◓ 63×44 / 1480-85 ▤ ○
Portrait of a Young Woman
Formerly Munich, Bernheim Collection
It was in the Seymour, London, Marcus Kappel and Noak, Berlin, Collections. Considered autograph by Bode, Schmarsow, Yashiro and L. Venturi; an old copy for Horne [1908] and A. Venturi [1925]; workshop, according to Van Marle and Gamba, possibly – according to Salvini – with final touches by Botticelli.

81 ⊞ ◓ 58×40 ▤ ○

78 A

Portrait of a Young Woman
Formerly Richmond, Cook Collection
Formerly in the Stirling Collection, London, as a portrait of Simonetta Vespucci. The traditional ascription to Botticelli was questioned by Cook [1902] and rejected by Horne [1908]. Considered autograph by Bode [1926], dating it c. 1478; Schmarsow

81

82

78 B

[1923], about 1475; and L. Venturi, 1490. The application of paint is not in Botticelli's usual manner.

82 ⊞ ◓ 45,2×31,8 / 1483* ▤ ⁝
Portrait of a Young Man
Washington, National Gallery of Art (Mellon Bequest)
It belonged to the Pourtalès and Schickler Collections, Paris; Duveen, Hamilton and Mackay, New York; Mellon, Washington. Reascribed to Botticelli by Berenson [1922], after long being attributed to Masaccio. The ascription is generally accepted, except for R. Fry [1926] and Mesnil. The tender coyness, rare or unknown in similar works by Botticelli, presages the affectionate sentimentality of the immediately following religious works. Dated between 1482 and 1487.

83 ⊞ ◓ diam. 84,5 ▤ ⁝
Madonna Nursing Christ, with Young St John and an Angel London, National Gallery
Left by Abbot Carlo Bianconi, Bologna, to a relative (1802), who sold it to the museum in 1855 as a work of Botticelli. On the back is the legend "M[aster(?)] Giuliano da San Ghallo," suggesting that Sangallo may have executed the original frame (lost), as he did for other paintings by Botticelli. Mesnil thinks it refers to the name of the owner. Degenhardt [1955] – after the old hypothesis of Richter [1898] – thinks Sangallo did the painting, but accepts the

87 (plates LX-LXI)

general Botticelli-style layout. Critics, since Ulmann [1893], do not consider the execution Botticelli's. There is a faithful copy in the Yerkers Collection, New York.

84 ⊞ ◓ diam. 118,5 ▤ ⁝
Madonna and Child with Young St John and two Angels Glasgow, Art Gallery and Museum
Generally ignored by scholars, but autograph for Spender [Museum Catalogue, 1945], who dates it 1481–4. A general sensitivity, as well as an

85 (plate XXII)

88

unsteady vibration, suggest the hand of a refined unknown artist.

85 ⊞ ◓ 58×39,5 / 1483* ▤ ⁝
Madonna and Child (Madonna of the Book)
Milan, Museo Poldi Pezzoli
Catalogued as Botticelli's since 1881. In 1890 Morelli

lamented the repainting and glazing, which were removed in 1951. Then all reservations ended about the authorship. A. Venturi [1913] had considered it workshop. Generally dated to 1481–5 (but, for Russoli [1955], 1480–90).

86 ⊞ ◉ diam. 118 *1483-85*

Madonna and Child with five Angels (Madonna of the Magnificat) Florence, Uffizi

Sold to the Uffizi in 1784 by Ottavio Magherini. The composition is framed in an unusual round window: under a crown of stars, surmounted by a golden halo with the Holy Spirit, sits Mary writing the *Magnificat*. Generally considered autograph after Cavalcaselle [1864]. Ulmann, Horne, A. Venturi, Gamba and Argan date it 1482; Yashiro and Van Marle, 1481; Bode, Schmarsow, L. Venturi and Bettini, 1485; Salvini, 1482–3. Despite the odd repaintings, wearing of glaze and other damage, particularly in the faces of the Madonna and Child, this author would date it about 1485.

The same subject in the Louvre, without the angel on the left, is probably workshop, as is that in the Pierpont Morgan Library, New York (perhaps from the Alessandrini house, Florence), albeit with variations; and a third, in the Swiss Federal warehouses, likewise variant, and cut into two octagonal pieces.

87 ⊞ ◉ 185 × 180 1485

Madonna and Child with the two Saints John (Bardi Madonna) Berlin, Staatliche Museen

Commissioned by Agnolo Bardi for the altar of his chapel in Sto Spirito, Florence, in late 1485; proved by the papers published by Supino [1899]: payment in February 1485 to Giuliano da Sangallo for the frame and final payment to Botticelli in August (comprising 35 florins for the work, 2 for gilding and 2 for ultramarine blue; Sangallo had 24 for the "ornament"). Identification of this work is confirmed by the descriptions of "Billi," the Anonimo Gaddiano and Vasari. It was taken to the Bardi house before 1677 and sold in 1825 to an antique dealer; acquired in 1829 by Rumohr for the museum. There is no information about the *predella* that accompanied it.

88 ⊞ ◉ ———

Madonna and Child

Formerly Berlin, Simon Collection

It came from the James Mann Collection, Scotland. A reworking of the figures of *The Bardi Madonna* (87); autograph for A. Venturi [1925] and others; workshop for Van Marle, Gamba and Salvini. A similar copy went from the Panciatichi-Ximenes Collection, Florence, to the Carmichael and then to the Benson Collection, London. Present whereabouts unknown.

83

84

86 (plates XXVI–XXVII)

Variant copy of 86 (Paris, Louvre)

Variant copy of 86 (New York, Pierpont Morgan Library)

89 (plate XXXVIII)

89 ⊞ ◉ diam. 143,5 1487*

Madonna and Child and six Angels (Madonna of the Pomegranate) Florence, Uffizi

From the collection of Cardinal de' Medici, it went to that of the Grand Dukes of Tuscany in 1675; and thence to the Uffizi in 1780. Horne [1908] suggested that it was the *tondo* commissioned by the magistrate of the Massai di Camera in 1487. Supporting this is the original frame, which is adorned with lilies confirming that it was painted for a public office, and the style, which would fit the period [Salvini]. Accepted by A. Venturi [1925], Gamba, Chastel [1957] and, with reservations, by Bettini [1958]; for Ulmann, it is earlier than 1480; Van Marle, 1480–1; Bode, followed by Schmarsow, Yashiro and L. Venturi [1937], c 1482. Originally richly gilded, the *tondo* now seems drab because of the loss of the gilding and the present opaqueness of the colors.

A workshop copy, with an additional angel, is in the Staatliche Museen, Berlin. Further copies of the central figures are in the Aynard Collection, Lyons, and, in fresco, in a chapel in Via Panicale, Florence. An adaptation, without two angels, formerly in the Julius Wernher Collection, is now in the Ludlow Collection, London.

90 ⊞ ◉ diam. 86,5

Madonna and Child with Young St John and an Angel Cincinnati, Edwards Collection

From the Salting Collection, London, it went (1885) to the Benson Collection, Philadelphia. Published by Fiocco [1930] as autograph of about 1487; a high-quality work, but Botticelli, according to this writer, did not execute it.

91 ⊞ ◉ diam. 192

Madonna and Child with six Angels Holding Candlesticks (Madonna of the Candelabra) Formerly Berlin, Kaiser Friedrich Museum

The traditional attribution to Botticelli was confirmed by Morelli [1893], while Meyer [1890] considered it largely workshop. Followed by many scholars, except Bode [1921 and 1926], who sees a large contribution by Botticelli. Destroyed in 1945 during the war. A workshop copy (70 × 40 cm.), with variations (Christ leans on a tipped column, perhaps of allegorical significance), is preserved in the town hall of Poppi (Casentino).

92 ⊞ ◉ diam. 110

Madonna Adoring Christ, with four Angels (Madonna of the Roses) Florence, Pitti

There are no modern attributions to Botticelli; generally ignored or ascribed to his school. Mentioned because Berenson considered it a copy of a lost original, in part

90

91

92

Variant copy of 92 (Baltimore, Museum of Art)

93

confirmed by the following painting.

Another copy (diam. 129·5 cm.), with five angels, in the Baltimore Museum of Art – once in the collection of Lady Louisa Ashburton – and then that of Henry Jacob, Baltimore, until 1935 – is attributed to the workshop of Berenson, but others [Hendy; Kuehnel] ascribe it to Botticelli and assistants.

93 ⊞ ◉ diam. 170 *1490

Madonna and Child with Young St John and six Angels Rome, Galleria Borghese

Joint work of Botticelli and his workshop [Berenson; Gamba], with the hasty addition of an outsized St John, which, according to Mesnil, recalls the resuscitated child painted by Filippino Lippi in the Church of the Carmine. Salvini, noting the high quality of the painting, ascribes it to the assistant who painted the Chantilly *Pomona* (70) and dates it about 1490.

A *tondo* (diam. 170 cm.) copy of the central figures, with landscape, formerly owned by Prince Mestchersky, Moscow, was fully described by Muratoff [*Starye Godye*, 1911]. Another, with Christ embracing the Madonna, St John already a youth, and an angel holding a book, was part of the Nardus Collection, Suresnes, and is mentioned only by Reinach.

The St Barnabas Altarpiece

Ordered from Botticelli by the consuls of the guild of *Medici e Speziali*, patrons of the Church of S. Barnaba, over the main altar of which the painting hung until 1700. Then it was transferred to the back wall and enlarged by Agostino Veracini's addition in 1717 of the arch and baldachin over the two *tondi* behind the throne. After the Napoleonic suppression of the church and monastery (1808), the panel was transferred to the Accademia and then (1919) to the Uffizi, where Veracini's additions were removed. Of the *predella*, originally comprizing seven sections and joined to the main panel until 1717, four sections have survived and are in the Uffizi, Florence. They are considered autograph by all, except Cavalcaselle [1864] and Bode [1921], who consider them workshop. The most likely dating, c. 1488 (or two years later), is supported by Gamba, Bettini, Argan and Salvini; 1486, for Mesnil and Chastel; 1482–3, for Horne, Bode, Schmarsow, Yashiro, and the two Venturis; about 1494, for Van Marle.

94 A ⊞ ◉ 268 × 280 *1490

Madonna and Child Enthroned with four Angels and six Saints

The saints are: Catherine of Alexandria, Augustine and

Reduced copy of 93 (formerly Moscow, Mestchersky Collection).

94 A (plates XLII-XLIII)

94 B

94 C

94 D

94 E

Barnabas, John the Baptist, Ignatius and Michael. The outer angels hold the baldachin of the throne and the others display the nails and the crown of thorns of the Passion. The two *tondi* behind the throne depict, in monochrome on a gold ground, the Archangel Michael and the Virgin of the Annunciation. On the step of the throne is a verse from Dante, "Virgin Mother, daughter of Your Son" [*Paradiso,* XXXIII, 1]. We have reproduced it here with Veracini's additions (see above) because they replaced essential elements that must have been removed from the original.

A copy of the Madonna and Child alone was in the Benson Collection, London, after it had gone from the Panciatichi-Ximenes Collection, Florence, to the Carmichael in London.

94 B ▦ ◓ 20×38 *1490 ▤ ⁝

The Vision of St Augustine
The second section of the *predella*. St Augustine, meditating on the mystery of the Trinity, sees a child who wants to transfer all the water from the sea into a small hole. To the saint's protestations of the impossibility of the feat, the child replies: "And how do you expect to transfer the immense mystery of the Trinity into your small brain?", and disappears. The literary source is universally acknowledged to be Jacopo da Voragine's *Legenda aurea*. For the other sections, see also the general discussion of the altarpiece.

94 c ▦ ◓ 21×41 *1490 ▤ ⁝

Christ of the Pietà
The fourth and middle section of the *predella*. In the lower right corner are minute figures of Calvary.

94 D ▦ ◓ 21×40.5 *1490 ▤ ⁝

Salome with the Head of John the Baptist
The fifth section of the *predella*. The bearded head, here used for the Baptist, was an iconographic element dear to Botticelli.

94 E ▦ ◓ 21×38 *1490 ▤ ⁝

The Removal of the Heart of St Ignatius
The sixth section of the *predella*. According to Pietro de' Natali's *Catalogus sanctorum*, Ignatius was tortured at Trajan's orders but refused to abjure his faith, asserting that Christ's name was written on his heart. After his death his heart was removed and the Redeemer's name was seen inscribed in gold letters.

95 ▦ ◓ diam. 147 ▤ ⁝

Madonna and Child with six Angels Bearing the Symbols of the Passion Florence, Galleria Corsini
In the seventeenth century it went from the Medici villa at Careggi to the Corsinis. It is probably a workshop variation of the St Barnabas Altarpiece (94), according to Horne and Salvini, who dates it c 1495. Altered by old repaintings, which make judgments difficult. A variant copy (88 × 64 cm.), with only two angels, went from the Constabili Collection, Ferrara, to the Musée Bonnat of Bayonne. Of good quality, it is considered by Berenson [1963], the only scholar to comment, to be a simple copy.

96 ▦ ◓ ▬▬ ▤ ⁝

Madonna and Child with Young St John Formerly Vienna, Lanckoronski Collection
This *tondo* panel went (c. 1890) to its last known owner from the Leclanché Collection. Considered a late autograph by Ulmann [1893], but more likely workshop, according to Van Marle and Salvini; not mentioned by other scholars.

A copy (tempera on panel, 124 × 85 cm.) went from the Bammeville Collection to the Barker, London, and (1895) to the Museum of Fine Arts, Boston. Generally ascribed to the workshop, except by Hendy [1932], who considers it an

Variant copy of 96 (Boston, Museum of Fine Arts)

99

autograph of 1480–5. Restored in 1930.

97 ▦ ◓ 47×29 1490* ▤ ⁝

Madonna and Child Rome, Galleria Colonna
Not mentioned by most scholars; for Van Marle, it is school of Botticelli; for Salvini, workshop, about 1490; for Gamba, autograph. Pleasantly executed but hard to judge because of damage and retouching. A copy (110 × 65 cm.) — varying in the addition of a parapet and vase of flowers in the foreground and a landscape with trees in the background — was sold by Durand-Ruel, Paris.

98 ▦ ◓ 79×88 ▤ ⁝

Madonna and Child El Paso (Texas), Museum of Fine Arts (Samuel H. Kress, Collection)
It went from the collection of the Count de Sarty to those of the Baron de Vendeuvre and of the Grassets, Paris; then to Duveen, who sold it to Samuel H. Kress. Autograph for A. Venturi [1924 and 1925], Berenson, Gamba, Chastel [1957] and the El Paso catalogers. Notwithstanding its quality, though, it seems to be of the school. The *tondo* seems irregularly cut, suggesting that the original shape was different.

99 ▦ ◓ diam. 68 *1490 ? ▤ ⁝

Madonna and Child with Young St John Formerly Rome, Lazzaroni Collection
Acquired about 1925 from the dealer Ehrich. Despite much retouching on the left and probable cutting down, Botticelli's hand can be recognized [Salvini], though not enough to make this absolutely autograph, as A. Venturi [1925 and 1926],

Variant copy of 99 (Montpellier, Musée Fabre).

Variant copy of 99 (Modena, Galleria Estense).

Reduced variant copy of 99 (New York, Duveen Property).

Reduced variant copy of 99 (Florence, Palazzo Vecchio).

Van Marle Gamba and Bettini believe. For Mesnil and Chastel [1957] it is workshop. Van Marle's and Mesnil's dating to c. 1490 seems more likely than c. 1483, advanced by Gamba and accepted by Bettini and Salvini. A slightly varied copy, until 1863 in the Campana Collection, is in the Musée Fabre, Montpellier. Another (diam. 68 cm.), set indoors, now in the Galleria Estense, Modena, came from the former Obizzi del Catajo Collection (1805) and is considered autograph by Castellani-Tarabini [1854] and S. Ricci [1925], though attributed correctly to the school by A. Venturi [1883], Van Marle, Yashiro, Zocca [1933], Gamba and Pallucchini [1945]. A third, rectangular copy (37 × 29 cm.) belongs to Duveen, New York, having been in the De Sarty, De Vendeuvre and Grasset Collections, Paris (the same history as 98, and the dimensions of the two pictures make it unlikely they could have been confused). Considered autograph by L. Venturi [1932] and Langton-Douglas [1941], while Mesnil and Salvini rightly attribute it to the workshop. A fourth copy (diam. 85 cm.), with the figures set between two windows opening onto a mountainous landscape, is in the Camera Verde of Palazzo Vecchio, Florence, and, according to the writing on the back, came from the Florentine tobacco factory of Sant'Orsola. Much damaged, but still ascribable to the workshop. An identical copy is in the Fitzwilliam Museum, Cambridge.

95

97

98

The St Mark Altarpiece

Commissioned about 1488 or not later than 1490 by the goldsmiths' guild for the Sant'Alò Chapel in S. Marco, Florence. Replaced in 1596 by a *Transfiguration* by G. B. Paggi, it was removed to the chapter, thence to the Accademia (1807) and finally to the Uffizi (1919), its present location. It preserves the original *predella* with five scenes on a single panel, generally accepted as autograph (except by Mesnil and Bettini, who see Filippino Lippi's hand in the execution). The *predella* is also of 1488–90. This dating was confirmed by documents discovered by Mesnil [1903] and Horne [1908].

100A ⊞ ◑ 378 × 258 ▤ ⫶
*1490

The Coronation of the Madonna and four Saints
The four saints depicted are John the Evangelist, Augustine, Jerome, and Eligius, patron saint of goldsmiths. The coronation is clearly inspired by Dante. The contribution of assistants is evident chiefly in the saints' robes and in the landscape. The altarpiece has been cut down slightly.

A variation (with donors)

101

103

in the John Bass Collection, New York, came from S. Giusto, Volterra, and is generally ascribed to the workshop. Despite damage and repainting, Berenson sees the hand of Bartolomeo di Giovanni. Another workshop copy (late copy for Yashiro) is in the Kunstmuseum, Basle.

100B ⊞ ◑ 21 × 269 ▤ ⫶
*1490
Sacred Scenes
The *predella* of the St Mark Altarpiece (see above). The scenes concern St John the Evangelist on Patmos, St Augustine in his cell, the Annunciation, St Jerome penitent, and the miracle of St Eligius. In this last scene, the patron saint of goldsmiths is working on the horse's hoof before restoring it to the animal. In the center is the woman whose nose the saint reattached.

101 ⊞ ◑ 86 × 60 ▤ ⫶
1490-95 ?
Madonna and Child
Formerly Paris, Trotti property It went from the castle of Trebbio to the Spencer Stanhope Collection, Florence; later it was sold (1922) in Paris as autograph by G. Rabit. The attribution, accepted by A. Venturi [1925], has been rejected by scholars since Van Marle ascribed it to the school and dated it 1490–5.

102 ⊞ ◑ 150 × 156 ▤ ⫶
1489 - 90
The Annunciation Florence, Uffizi
According to the *Libro* of the benefactors of the convent of Cestello in Pinti, this picture

Central part of the predella, *100.*

was commissioned from Botticelli, about 14 May 1489, by Benedetto di ser Giovanni Guardi, for the chapel of the Cestello church (Sta Maria Maddalena de' Pazzi); the artist was paid 30 ducats. The picture was rediscovered in 1870 in a house at Fiesole belonging to the nuns of Sta Maria Maddalena de' Pazzi and went to the Uffizi two years later. Autograph for Ulmann, Bode [1921 and 1926], A. Venturi [1925], L. Venturi [1937] and Mesnil. For others it is a collaboration between Botticelli and the workshop or, according to Bettini [1942], between Botticelli and Filippino Lippi. The picture is in its original frame, which contains a small *Pietà,* probably workshop [Salvini].

In a copy (panel, 106 × 115 cm.) formerly in Berlin, Kaiser Friedrich Museum and destroyed in World War II, Mesnil thought he identified the contribution of Botticelli, but it was most likely a workshop copy.

100 A

100 B

102 (plates L-LI)

103 ⊞ ◍ 37,5×25,5 🗒 ⁞

Christ and Young St John
(?) Ottawa, National Gallery of
Canada
Acquired in 1927 from the
dealer Böhler, Lucerne.
Autograph for A. Venturi,
Bode (dating it 1490—4),
Yashiro (dating it c. 1487) and
Van Marle (suggesting 1485–
90). More probably workshop
according to Berenson,
Gamba, Salvini and Collobi
Ragghianti [1949], who
considers it a fragment of a
Venus with Cupids.

104 ⊞ ◍ ——— 🗒 ⁞

**Pietà with Saints Francis
and Jerome** Kaliningrad
(Königsberg), State Museum
From Berlin. Berenson
attributed it to the workshop;
Rajackrizn considers it
autograph [*Vrade Iskustvo*,
1960]; ignored by others.
A variation (with the Madonna
and St John, and a *pentimento*
in the position of Christ's arms),

105

106

in the Soprintendenza alle
Gallerie, Florence, was
ascribed by Berenson to the
school.

105 ⊞ ◍ 57×38 🗒 ⁞

Portrait of a Youth Paris,
Louvre
It went from the Frizzoni Salis
to the Hainauer Collection,
Berlin, then to the Schlichting
Collection, Paris, and finally
to the Louvre. Attribution has
been controversial; recently
reascribed to Botticelli by
Collobi Ragghianti [1949], and
dated c. 1485, but rejected by
Salvini. Perhaps the work of
Mariano d'Antonio under
supervision of Botticelli.

106 ⊞ ◍ 49×35 🗒 ⁞
1490*

**Portrait of Michele
Marullo** Barcelona, H. Cambó
de Guardans Collection
In the possession of the Duke
of Leuchtenberg, St Petersburg,
in the nineteenth century, it
was on a larger panel and was
attributed to Masaccio. Then
it passed to the Simon
Collection, Berlin (1906),
where F. Laban [1906]
recognized it as a Botticelli.
Berenson identified the subject:
Michele Marullo, known as
Taraniota, Greek, Humanist,
man of letters and soldier.
He was a guest of the Medicis
from 1489 to 1494 and
returned to Florence a second
time in 1496 to marry the poet
Alessandra Scala. He left again
in 1500 and drowned a short
time later when fording the
Cecina. His wife withdrew to a
convent and survived him by
only a few years. The picture
may date from his first stay in
Florence [Salvini].

*Variant copy of 102 (formerly
in Berlin, Kaiser Friedrich
Museum).*

107 ⊞ ◍ 49×37 🗒 ⁞
1490*

**Portrait of Lorenzo
Lorenzano** Philadelphia,
Pennsylvania Museum
Sold by the Lazzaronis, Paris,
to the Johnsons, Philadelphia,
who gave it to the museum.
Lorenzano, a Florentine scholar
of the Medici court, held the
chair of dialectics at Pisa, and
then that of physics and
medicine. He died in 1502,
when in a fit of madness he
threw himself down a well.
Generally considered autograph
and dated about 1490, or just
after, except for Yashiro [1929],
who dates it to 1487. Poor
state of preservation.

108 ⊞ ◍ 100×178 🗒 ⁞
1490*

**The Coronation of the
Madonna with four Saints**
New York, Metropolitan
Museum
The saints are Anthony the
Abbot and John the Baptist,
left, and Miniatus and Francis,
right. It went from the Burne-
Jones, London, to the Cassirer
Collection, Berlin, then to Von
Lichnowski, Kuchelne
(Austria), and finally to Julius
Bache, New York, who left it to
the museum. Generally
considered autograph, but it
may be a copy of a lost
original painted by Botticelli to
help his brother Giovanni and
destined for a church or a
chapel in San Miniato,
Florence. This possibility
emerges from the present
author's examination of the
archives of the chapter of the
Florentine cemetery of
Ognissanti. In the Madonna

there is that sense of rhythm
and soft abandon that
characterizes Botticelli's work
after 1490, the dating suggested
by Gamba, Bettini and
Salvini.

109 ⊞ ◍ diam. 84 🗒 ⁞
1490*

**Madonna and Child with
Young St John**
Williamstown, Sterling Clark
Museum
Formerly in the collection of
H. de Triqueti, Paris, who left it
to his daughter Bianca Lee
Childe; then in the Nolleva
Collection (1886); then sold

107

*Variant copy of 104 (Florence,
Soprintendenza alle Gallerie).*

by Charpentier (Paris,
December 1951). Autograph,
about 1490 (according to
Longhi, Gamba and Salvini),
except for the young St John,
who seems a later addition.

110 ⊞ ◍ 89,5×73,5 🗒 ⁞
1490*

**Madonna and Child with
Young St John** Dresden,
Gemäldegalerie
A revival of a theme of his
youth and executed in that
"affectionate" spirit peculiar to
Botticelli toward the end of the
century. The idea is certainly
Botticelli's. As for the
execution, autograph for
Morelli [1891], Jähnig [1929],
Gamba and Salvini; workshop
for Ulmann, A. Venturi, Van
Marle, Berenson and Mesnil.
The quality of the painting
suggests Botticelli's execution,
which might be the original of a
series of well-known
variations. Compare, for
example, the version (81 × 66·5
cm.) in Palazzo Vecchio,
Florence (Sala di Penelope), in
which Cirri [1966] suggests

that Botticelli may have had a
hand. The following works are
certainly replicas: the panel
(90 × 71 cm.), formerly Ruth
Buller Collection, Duisburg,
which came from the Vernon
Watney Collection, London,
and was sold by Christie's in
1966; another, without the
young St John, in the
Städelsches Kunstinstitut,
Frankfurt. A third (94 × 62·5
cm.), also without the St John,
replaced by an open window
showing a river landscape, was
formerly in the Ginori house,
then the property of the Prince
of Liechtenstein, and is now in
the Aldo Crespi Collection,
Milan. Similar to this is a panel
(83 × 65 cm) that went to the
National Gallery, London
(1867) from the Florentine
hospital of Sta Maria Nuova.
which had received it as a gift
(1863) from Count Galli Tassi. It
is considered autograph by
Frizzoni [1879], Ulmann and
others. The same variations
mark two other panels, one in
the Musée des Beaux-Arts,
Lille (63 × 47 cm), formerly
at Capodimonte, brought to
France with the Napoleonic
booty (1803) and installed at
Lille in 1873; the other in the
H. T. G. Collection, Oxford
(80 × c. 60 cm.). Related to
these is a *tondo* (diam. 120
cm.) in Palazzo Chigi Saracini,
Siena, with two angels instead
of St John, probably painted
about 1540 which means it
cannot even be of the school of
Botticelli. But some have
recognized in it the same
artist responsible for the known
workshop paintings. Finally,
there are replicas of the
Madonna and Child alone in the
Arthur Severn Collection,
London (with a Gothic castle
in the background) and in that
of L. Harris, London (with a
naked *putto*).

*Reduced copy of 110 (London,
National Gallery).*

*Variant copy of 110 (Siena,
Chigi Saracini Collection).*

109

110

111

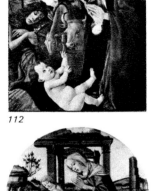

113

112

111 ⊞ ⊘ diam. 115 1490-1500 ▤ ⁚

Madonna and Child with three Angels Florence, Pitti
The two angels behind are Michael and Gabriel. Workshop, though Botticelli probably applied finishing touches, according to Gamba. Painted in 1490, or 1500 at the latest [Chastel].

In the Sulzbach Collection, Paris, there was a rectangular panel duplicating the Madonna and Child, adored by the young St John, to the right, in a delicate loggia opening onto a landscape.

112 ⊞ ⊘ 46×41 1490-95* ▤ ⁚

Madonna and Young St John Adoring Christ Edinburgh, National Gallery of Scotland
From the Fuller Maitland Collection. Fragment of a larger work, considered autograph by A. Venturi [1925] and Salvini, dating it about 1485 (though it seems much later); largely autograph for Berenson [1932]; workshop for Van Marle, Gamba and Mesnil.

113 ⊞ ⊘ diam. 94 ▤ ⁚

Madonna and Young St John Adoring Christ London, National Gallery
Acquired from the Patrizis, Rome, by Salting, who gave it to the gallery in 1910. Autograph for Ulmann [1893]; ascribed to the workshop by Van Marle, Mesnil, Davies [1951] and Salvini. Another version (diam. 115 cm.), that passed through the collections of Lord Grimthorpe, Fairfax-Murray and Cassel, all in England, and then to the American collection of De Navarro, Glen Head – frequently exhibited as autograph, at the Royal Academy, London, the Caracas Museum, University of Mexico, Palacio de Belas Artes in Ciudad Trujillo and the Palazzo Reale, Milan – seems to have been painted much later than the period in which the style of Botticelli continued in vogue, as is indicated by the technique, which is quite different from that of Botticelli, his workshop and contemporary imitators. Another replica (diam. 90 cm.), with the addition of St Joseph, which Lord Ward bought (1847) in Rome from the Counts of Bisenzo and then passed (1892) to Deprez, to Wickham Flower (1893), Agnew (1904), is now in Lord Faringdon's Collection at Buscot Park. Although Waagen [1854] considered it a very late autograph, it is workshop according to Berenson and Gebhardt. In a third version, likewise *tondo*, in the Ocampo Collection, Paris, the Madonna kneels in front of a pillar of huge blocks, the naked Christ on the ground stretches His arms to her, and the young Baptist stands over Him; to the sides is a mountain landscape with rivers. It may be the prototype of the De Navarro version. Nevertheless it is workshop, without Botticelli's

119

120 (plate XL)

collaboration, or perhaps the work of a follower no longer under Botticelli's direct influence.

114 ⊞ ⊘ 1478 ▤ ⁝

Hanged Men Formerly Florence, The old Palazzo del Bargello
The hanged men depicted were the Pazzis and others who conspired against the Medicis, whom Botticelli was commissioned to paint for the Porta della Dogana in the old Bargello of Florence (next to Palazzo Vecchio) in 1478 (see *Outline Biography*). They were painted out in 1494.

115 ⊞ ⊘ 150×130 ▤ ⁝

The Baptism of Christ Formerly Faenza, Guidi Collection Sold in Rome in 1902 when Sangiorgi sold the collection of the Counts Guidi of Faenza. It was then that A. Venturi judged it a late autograph, though much damaged. Autograph, too, for Ragghianti [1954]; workshop for Gamba and Salvini. Further judgments cannot be made because the picture's present location is unknown.

117

116

116 ⊞ ⊘ 46×37 1490-95* ▤ ⁚

Madonna and Child Adored by Young St John New York, John D. Rockefeller Collection
It went from the Charles Somerwell (1884) to the J. P. Heseltine Collection, London. Considered autograph by Ulmann [1893], who dated it c 1482, and by Yashiro [1929], Van Marle, Berenson and Gamba, who date it c. 1491; workshop for Horne [1908], Bode [1921 and 1926], Mesnil and Salvini, who thinks Botticelli added final touches. Certain fine touches anticipate the admirable *St Augustine* in Florence (120).

A close copy of the Madonna and Child alone, against a dark background, was formerly in the Colnaghi Collection, London, and is now in the Esk Collection, London.

117 ⊞ ⊘ diam. 85 1495* ▤ ⁚

Madonna and Child with Young St John New York, Duveen Property
Formerly in the Bauer and Schaeffer collections, Frankfurt, and the Leyland Collection, Woolton Hall, Liverpool. Exhibited many

times as autograph and so considered by Berenson, Langton-Douglas and M. W. Brockwell, who date it to the end of the century. Workshop version of Botticelli's idea for Mesnil and Salvini.

A single variant replica – including a balustrade in the foreground – is in a private collection in Rome; executed between 1490 and 1495, according to Mesnil.

118 ⊞ ⊘ diam. 112 ▤ ⁚

Reversed copy of 119 (Birmingham, Barber Institute).

Madonna and Child with two Angels Vienna, Akademie der bildenden Künste
From the Canigiani house, Florence; acquired by the Prince of Liechtenstein, who gave it to the Vienna gallery about 1890.

Autograph for Ulmann; workshop for Horne [1908] and Van Marle; school for Salvini; probably executed by the same follower who worked on the Uffizi *Annunciation* (102).

119 ⊞ ⊘ 134×92 1495* ▤ ⁚

Madonna and Child Embraced by Young St John Florence, Pitti
The traditional attribution to Botticelli, supported by old inventories, is accepted by Ulmann [1893], Bode [1921 and 1926], Schmarsow [1923], Bettini and Salvini, who date it 1490–1500. It is workshop for Morelli [1886], A. Venturi [1925], Berenson [1932], Gamba and Mesnil. Yet there is a high degree of that soft and affectionate treatment of line characteristic of Botticelli at the end of the century, in fact, the full development of that *mouvementé* and compact composition. It is hard to decide about the execution because of damage and much retouching. A replica (panel, 40 × 30 cm.) formerly in the Dreyfus Collection, Paris, was published as partially autograph by Reinach [1906 and 1918], and accepted by Guiffrey [1908]. Gebhardt [1908] considers it entirely autograph and considered it the prototype of the Uffizi

103

121

of Ignazio Hugford to that of Piero Pieralli, who sold it to the Uffizi in 1779. Here again is that careful sense of small detail of the two Judith panels (38 A and B) and that youthful diligence of a gold-smith in the decoration, a foretaste of the *Madonna under a Baldachin* (128) and *The Calumny of Apelles* (127). Universally accepted as autograph (though L. Venturi [1931] also sees the hands of the miniaturists Gherardo and Monte di Fora), while the dating varies between 1490 and 1500.

121 ⊞ ◐ 24×36 / 1495* 🗐 ⁝

The Annunciation New York, Robert Lehman Collection
It went from the Barberini Collection, Rome, to the Huldschinsky Collection, Berlin, and thence to New York. Morelli [1893], Horne [1908] and A. Venturi [1925] consider it workshop; autograph for Ulmann [1893], Bode [1906], Schmarsow, Van Marle, Yashiro [1929], L. Venturi [1931], Gamba and Salvini, with dates between

1474 and 1500. This small delicate painting revives a youthful theme with a more vibrant sense of line and greater pictorial density.

122 ⊞ ◐ 34,3×25,5 / 1495* 🗐 ⁝

The Communion of St Jerome New York, Metropolitan Museum (Altman Bequest)
The subject comes from the apocryphal *Epistle of the Blessed Eusebius* published in Venice and Messina in 1473 and in Florence in 1490. The picture belonged to Gino Capponi in the nineteenth century and then to his heirs, the marquises Farinola, who had it cleaned. Subsequently acquired by Benjamin Altman, it went to the museum about 1915. It is probably the *"Transito di san Girolamo di mano di Sandro"* which Francesco del Pugliese had first intended for the chapel of the castle of Sommaia, which he had acquired in 1488. In his later will he left it to his cousin Niccolò di Piero del Pugliese. Horne's hypothesis, that the painting went from Francesco del Pugliese to Piero

makes exact judgment difficult.

123A ⊞ ◐ 176×163 🗐 ⁝

Madonna Enthroned with Christ Blessing between four Saints
The saints are Sebastian, Lawrence, John the Evangelist, and Roch. Much damage and repainting have considerably altered the figure of Christ, among others. In the seventeenth century the sides were mutilated when it was fitted with a new frame.

123B ⊞ ◐ 14,5×163 🗐 ⁝

Sacred Scenes and Figures
The *predella* comprises four *tondi* with saints and central *tondo* of the *Pietà;* together with two episodes from the life of St Lawrence (*Distribution of Treasures to the Poor* and *Martyrdom*) and two anachronistic decorative elements that were probably painted over two other scenes.

124 ⊞ ◐ diam. 59,6 / 1495* 🗐 ⁝

Madonna Adoring Christ Washington, National Gallery of Art (Samuel H. Kress Bequest)

124   125

122

canvas. Workshop for Berenson and Van Marle; school for Salvini. Another copy, reversed, probably from the same cartoon (the dimensions of the figures in the two works are the same) went from the Donaldson Collection, Brighton, to the Barber Institute, Birmingham, where S. Spender [1945] considered it an autograph of 1487, though it is ignored by other scholars.

120 ⊞ ◐ 41×27 / 1495* 🗐 ⁝

St Augustine in his Cell Florence, Uffizi
Behind St Augustine is a fine monochrome *tondo* of the Madonna and Child. At his feet notes and goose quills in a happily "improvised" disorder. Vasari mentioned it as being in the house of Bernardo Vecchietti, attributing it to Filippo Lippi; Borghini admired it at the Vecchietti house in 1584. It reappeared in the early eighteenth century and passed from the Florentine collection

123 A

in 1502, has been accepted by the museum cataloguers. It is universally considered auto-graph; dating varies between 1490 and 1500.

A replica belongs to the Marchioness Negrotto Cambiaso, Genoa (35 × 25 cm.); another replica, which may simply be an old copy, was formerly in the Abdy Collection, Paris, and is now in the Benson Collection, London. A third, with variations in the details, belongs to A. Kay, formerly London, now New York.

The Montelupo Altarpiece

This work is so called because it is in the Church of S. Giovanni Evangelista in Montelupo Fiorentino. Published as autograph by Mesnil [1900], but later ascribed to the school, by other scholars as well. Gamba believes Botticelli put the final touches. Extensive repainting

Formerly in Paris, first in the Paravey Collection and then in the Reynaud Collection. Wildenstein bought it for 1,800,000 francs at an auction at the Hôtel Drouot (1929) and took it to America. Autograph for A. L. Mayer [1930], Van Marle, L. Venturi [1933] and Salvini. The dating varies between 1481 [Venturi] and 1490–1 [Mayer; Salvini], though it would seem even later.

125 ⊞ ◐ diam. 76 🗐 ⁝

Nativity Boston, Isabella Stewart Gardner Museum
Purchased early in the twentieth century from the Duke of Brindisi in Florence. Botticelli's hand seems evident in the Madonna, according to Van Marle and Mesnil. The rest is not merely workshop [Horne; Berenson; Salvini], but there even seem to be elements of Signorelli [Gamba], or extensive restoration by Vasari, or a composition of various elements by a good anonymous painter. Nevertheless Ulmann and Gamba considered it autograph.

126 ⊞ ◐ 127×125,1 🗐 ⁝

The Holy Family Raleigh (North Carolina), Museum of

123 B

Art (Samuel H. Kress Collection) In the background one can see the Three Kings approaching. Until the recent restoration the picture seemed to be set in a nocturnal landscape. It was in the J. F. Austen Collection, Horsmonden (Kent) from at least 1893 until 1921, when it was sold at Christie's to the Earl of Crawford and Balcarres, London. Kress acquired it in 1956. From 1893 it was considered autograph, and this view was accepted by Bode [1926], Van Marle and (albeit with collaborators) Cartwright [1956]. Berenson ascribed it to the workshop

127 (plates LII-LV)

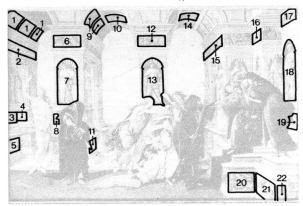

Scheme for identification of subsidiary representations in 127.

after Reinach and Gebhardt had attributed it to the school and Yashiro to an imitator. The *tondo* is imperfectly cut.

127 62×91 1495*

The Calumny of Apelles
Florence, Uffizi
Painted for Antonio Segni; it was seen in his son Fabio's house by Vasari [1550]. Then it went to Palazzo Pitti and finally to the Uffizi (1773). The subject – depicted by Apelles, to vindicate himself from the lies that his rival Antiphylos told King Ptolemy Philelphos, in a painting described by Lucian in the *De calumnia* – was very popular in the fifteenth century, both from the Latin text and Alberti's description (*De pictura*, III). Botticelli followed Lucian's text, which is richer in detail than L. B. Alberti's account. King Midas, with the ass's ears of the Bad Judge, sits on his throne between Ignorance and Suspicion and extends his hand to Envy, who leads Calumny. Guile and Deceit weave flowers in Calumny's hair, and she drags the calumnied. Penitence follows, turning to Naked Truth. The scene is set in a classical building

adorned with statues and gilded low reliefs representing (see numbers in plan below): (1) three episodes of the Novella of Nastagio degli Onesti (see 74); (2) the slaying of the centaurs; (3) Hercules and Lychas; (4) Apollo and Daphne; (5) Trajan's justice; (6) Bacchus finding Ariadne [Gamba] or Mars and Venus [Horne]; (7) David [Horne] or Theseus [Gamba]; (8) David and Goliath; (9) Mucius Scaevola; (10) St George and the Dragon; (11) the judgment of Paris; (12) cupids with the arms of Mars and a lion; (13) St George [Horne] or Mars [Gamba] in the same pose as Pippo Spano frescoed by Andrea del Castagno in Sant'Apollonia, Florence; (14) the fall of the Titans; (15) the slaying of the centaurs; (16) the myth of Prometheus [Salvini]; (17) Judith putting the head of Holofernes in a bag; (18) Judith; (19) Judith returning to Bethulia; (20) the centaur family, after a painting by Zeuxis described by Lucian; (21) Jupiter and Antiope; (22) Minerva with the gorgon's head. The ornate architecture may reflect some Humanist

setting, of the type for which Botticelli himself painted "many pictures surrounded by walnut railings and backboards, with many lively and beautiful figures" [Vasari]. It is also possible that these painted "episodes" were derived from paintings by Botticelli or his workshop. Otherwise it would be difficult to account for the assimilation of classical themes with stories from the Old Testament and from Boccaccio. This would suggest that the picture was painted in reaction to some calumny against Botticelli rather than Savonarola, as Landsberger [1933] thinks, and perhaps to enlighten Piero de' Medici, whose weak character was susceptible to various influences. It appears that the original frame bore these verses – attributed by Vasari to Fabio, the son of Antonio Segni – *Indicio quemquam ne falso laedere tentent// terrarum reges, parva tabella monet.//Huic similem Aegypti regi donavit Apelles:// rex fuit et dignus munere, munus eo.* Scholars all attribute the work to Botticelli's maturity; Bode suggests 1485–1490; Yashiro, Ulmann and, with less certainty, Salvini suggest 1490–1; Horne, both Venturis, Gamba, Bettini, Mesnil and Argan believe 1494–5; Salvini even considers possible the date of 1496, the year in which Lucian's works were published in Florence (though Botticelli seems to have known the texts from manuscript codices), or 1497, the year Savonarola was excommunicated. This last dating is also advanced by Landsberger.

128 diam. 65 1495*

Madonna and Child with three Angels (Madonna under a Baldachin) Milan, Pinacoteca Ambrosiana
Little is known about this sensitive and subtle masterpiece: It may be – as Horne [1908] supposed, followed by Gamba – that "little *tondo* from his [Botticelli's] hand that can be seen in the chamber of the prior of the Angeli in Florence, with small figures, but extremely gracious and made with beautiful care" mentioned by Vasari. The monastery of Sta Maria degli Angeli, in Via degli Alfani in Florence, was suppressed in 1808.

126

128 (plate LVI)

129 A

129 B

129 C

129 D

It is not known how the picture reached its present location. On the upper border of the baldachin, beneath the laurel, are barely decipherable gold letters (perhaps an S, an M, and an F), interlaced letters, a caduceus or plain interlace and palmettes. They may mean "Sandro di Mariano Filipepi" and allude to his evolution from pagan Humanism to the Christian Mystery, or they may refer to a gift that Charles VIII of France made to the Duke of Milan, or they may be simply a reinforcement of the scene by initials and symbols. The painting, traditionally attributed to Botticelli, is unanimously dated just after 1490.

Figures of Saints

There are four paintings, originally on panel but transferred to canvas, that belonged to the Stroganoff Collection, St Petersburg. With the Revolution they were

assigned to the Hermitage. They must have been the wings that Francesco del Pugliese commissioned for a *Last Judgment* by Fra Angelico for the Dominicans of S. Marco, Florence. Considered autograph by Hark [1896], Benois [1901] and Lazareff [1924]. Subsequently only the first two were considered autograph (129 A and B) [A. Venturi, 1927; Yashiro, 1929; Van Marle; Gamba; Bazin, 1957; Malizkaya, 1963]. The preciosity of color and the highly sensitive application of paint in *Gabriel* and *The Virgin Annunciate* confirm this thesis (although there may have been collaboration in secondary details). L. Venturi [1912], Mesnil and Salvini assign all four to the workshop.

129 A 45×13

The Archangel Gabriel
Moscow, Pushkin Museum

131

132

The People of Many Lands *and* Pentecost: *drawing (Darmstadt, Kupferstichkabinett) usually considered autograph; perhaps related to 132 or [Argan] 139.*

133

134

129ʙ ⊞ ✛ ⁴⁵×¹³ ▤ ⋮

The Virgin Annunciate
Moscow, Pushkin Museum

129c ⊞ ✛ ⁴⁵×²⁶ ▤ ⋮

St Jerome Penitent
Leningrad, Hermitage

129ᴅ ⊞ ✛ ⁴⁵×²⁶ ▤ ⋮

St Dominic Blessing
Leningrad, Hermitage

130 ⊞ ✛ ⁴⁹,⁵×³² ▤ ⋮

St Francis and Angel Musicians London, British Museum
The gold ground is finely worked, but there is much repainting and it is hard to judge. Therefore Berenson considered it a copy. The museum inventories record it as autograph and date it about 1495.

131 ⊞ ✛ ²⁸×³⁸ / 1495* ▤ ⋮

The Transfiguration and Saints Jerome and Augustine Rome, Pallavicini Collection
The old attribution of De Nicola was accepted by A. Venturi, Yashiro, Van Marle, Gamba and Bettini and dated to 1495–1500. For Mesnil, the work of imitators. For Salvini, it is a drawing of Botticelli, hurriedly and carelessly colored by the workshop, about 1490–5. Damaged and repainted.

132 ⊞ ✛ ²²¹×²²⁹ ▤ ⋮

Pentecost Greenville (South Carolina), Bob Jones University Formerly in the Gamberini (1872), Abbé Hyères (1874) and Cook, Richmond, collections; acquired in 1958 by Julius Weitzen and transferred to Greenville the following year. Known to Ulmann [1893], who ascribed it to the workshop, and followed by Bode [1921], A. Venturi [1925], Van Marle (who ascribed the execution to Raffaellino del Garbo), Berenson, Gamba, Mesnil, who considered the idea Botticelli's. This hypothesis was accepted by Salvini and Bettini (who also thought that Botticelli started the actual painting). Later Bode decided it was autograph [1926]. This writer believes there are other possibilities: it may be the central part of an altarpiece showing in the lower register every man understanding others' speech on the day of Pentecost (Acts 2:5–13), and in the upper part, perhaps in the form of a lunette, Christ and God blessing the descent of the Holy Spirit. Or the picture may be a replica of a smaller *tondo*, now lost, but with the three episodes mentioned above. As it is, the panel bears signs of having been cut above and below, and the composition that remains seems to be more suited to a circular than a rectangular composition.

133 ⊞ ✛ ⁴²×¹³⁶ ▤ ⋮

Five Allegorical Figures
Florence, Galleria Corsini
Mesnil is altogether convinced that this ornamental panel is

130

135 (plates LVIII–LIX)

autograph, while Yashiro and Reinach are probably right in attributing it to the workshop.

134 ⊞ ✛ ¹¹⁰×²⁰⁷ / 1495* ▤ ⋮

Pietà Munich, Alte Pinakothek
This picture, as Mesnil showed [1914], comes from the Church of S. Paolino, Florence. Acquired by Prince Ludwig of Bavaria just after the Uffizi restoration of 1813; state property since 1850. Most scholars consider it autograph, or at least largely autograph (though Struter [1903], Berenson, Horne and Van Marle ascribe it to the workshop), and date it between 1490 and 1500. The pose of Christ is exactly like that of one of the sinners in the ice in the drawing for Canto XXXIII of Dante's *Inferno* (see also 135).

135 ⊞ ✛ ¹⁰⁷×⁷¹ / 1495* ▤ ⋮

Pietà Milan, Museo Poldi Pezzoli
This is usually identified – after Von Hadeln's suggestion [1906] – with the panel Vasari saw [1568] in Sta Maria Maggiore, Florence, "in the chapel of the Panciatichis, very beautiful." Evidently the panel hung on a pillar, which would account for the fact that this panel is vertical rather than oblong like the Munich panel (134). Other scholars have thought the Munich panel is the one referred to by Vasari, but the Milan one was still in the sacristy of Sta Maria Maggiore in 1755. The Poldi Pezzoli acquired it in 1855. The 1951 restoration of the painting fully revealed the Botticellian tension of the line and the qualities of the painting,

carried out rapidly with such delicate *impasti* that one can still see the holes from the transposed cartoon (see Plate LIX, twice actual size).
Before this restoration doubts on the authorship were advanced by such scholars as Morelli, Frizzoni, Horne, A. Venturi, Berenson, L. Venturi and Mesnil. Since the restoration the work has been accepted [from Russoli, Museum Catalogue, 1955, to Argan and Salvini]. Dating varies from 1490 to 1500.
A replica (107 × 69·5 cm.), which went from the Bourgeois Collection, Cologne, to the Bautier, Brussels, was judged partially autograph by Mesnil [1914 and 1938], but considered a copy by Horne [1908] and Salvini. The unjustified variation in the Magdalene's robe and the inharmonious heavy color would suggest that it was not even supervised by Botticelli.

136 ⊞ ✛ ⁴⁷×³³ ▤ ⋮

The Redeemer Blessing
Bergamo, Accademia Carrara
Left to the Accademia by Morelli, who considered it autograph [1890], followed by A. Venturi [1925], who dated it about 1500, and Berenson [1932]. For other scholars, beginning with Ulmann, a diligent workshop treatment of

136

Variant painted copy of 136 (Cambridge, Mass., Fogg Art Museum).

the same subject in Detroit (66). Damaged and much repainted on the right side, from the hair to the wrist. A canvas replica (57·15 × 35 cm.) – perhaps a procession standard – in the Fogg Art Museum,

137

Cambridge, Mass., was considered autograph by Van Marle [1928 and 1931], while Mesnil thought there was a northern European cast in it that removed it from Botticelli's sphere. Another replica (70 × 48 cm.), with variations (Christ with the crown of thorns holds the point of the spear), was in the Lazzaroni Collection, Paris; it was probably painted in the work-shop after 31 May, 1492, when the holy spear given by Sultan Bayezid to Pope Innocent VIII was put on display [Mesnil].

137 ⊞ ⊕ 36,5×35 1495* 🗏 ⋮

Annunciation with a Devout Lady Hannover, Niedersächsische Landesgalerie
This came from the M. Kestner Collection. Considered late autograph by A. Venturi [1921 and 1925], Van Marle, Berenson [1932], Gamba and Mesnil (who thought it was quickly painted), Argan and Salvini (who dated it about 1498). Similar in composition to the drawing of the same subject that Botticelli did for Canto X of Dante's *Purgatorio*.

138A ⊞ ⊕ diam. 15 🗏 ⋮

The Archangel Gabriel of the

Annunciation Formerly Florence, Galleria Corsini
This picture and the one below were probably part of a *predella*. Both are autograph for Ulmann [1893], A. Venturi [1924 and 1925] (dating them to the end of the century), Yashiro (c. 1483), Van Marle (c. 1485–90) and Gamba. Mesnil and Salvini (who considers them a derivation from 137) ascribe them to the workshop.

138B ⊞ ⊕ diam. 15 🗏 ⋮

The Virgin of the Annunciation Formerly Florence, Galleria Corsini
See description above.

The irreparable state of 138A and 138B makes it necessary to reproduce the old and incomplete photographs above.

139 ⊞ ⊕ 47×41 1495* 🗏 ⋮

Derelicta Rome, Rospigliosi Collection
Among the many identifications of subject advanced, the most likely [Creizenach, 1898] concerns Tamar, ill-used and driven out by her half-brother Amnon. According to the passage in the version of the Bible then in use in Florence (II Samuel: 13), Tamar's robes, in the foreground, were a single reddish colour, not ornamented as rendered in later translations. When the picture was acquired (1816) by the Rospigliosis as a work of Masaccio (nothing is known of earlier owners), the subject was thought to be Rhea Silvia. Scholars saw it as a symbol of distress [Zola, 1896] or sorrow [Reinach]; Truth – the mother Virtue – driven out by Ignorance with her daughter's clothes (supposedly related to a Mantegna print, in which Truth is transformed into a tree) [Piccoli, 1930]; a Christian prisoner waiting to be devoured by wild beasts [Lesser, 1930]; Justice weeping for the death of Savonarola [Landsberger, 1933]; Virtue separated from Wisdom (or Divine Revelation) [Argan, 1956]. Biblical interpretations also include Ephraim's concubine after the

violence she was subjected to by the sons of Belial [A. Venturi, 1896], or Queen Vashti repudiated by Ahasuerus [Horne; Gamba; Bettini], or Mordecai inveighing before the palace of Ahasuerus [Wind, 1940–1; Berti and Baldini]; in the classical world, Lucretia violated by Tarquin, after Ovid (*Fasti*, II, 721–852) [Antonie-wicz, 1905]. The usual title of *Derelicta* goes back to Steinmann [1898]. It was A. Venturi who attributed the picture to Botticelli, followed by many later scholars, though it has been assigned to Filippino Lippi [Antoniewicz; Gamba, 1930, though he changed his mind later], Francesco di Giorgio [Hartlaub, 1910], Ercole de' Roberti [Lesser, 1930], and even to an English Pre-Raphaelite (an opinion that had currency about 1930). Chastel, while accepting the attribution to Botticelli, suggests that the picture is related to the *cassoni* depicting stories of illustrious women formerly in the Torrigiani house and certainly painted by Filippino Lippi (see 144). This hypothesis has a long history and in deference to it Gamba (followed by Mesnil) dates the picture about 1476; Bettini, 1481–2; Berti and Baldini, about 1480. Other datings: just before 1490 [Bode], about 1483 [Yashiro], about 1490 [Argan]. Venturi (followed by Salvini) dated it about 1495, which seems the most likely.

140 ⊞ ⊕ 36×27 1495* 🗏 ⋮

Judith with the Head of Holofernes Amsterdam, Rijksmuseum
Acquired at the beginning of the twentieth century by Richard von Kauffmann, Berlin, from the Butterys of London. It then went to the Königs, who sold it to Van Rath in 1930, on whose death (1941) the museum inherited it. Universally accepted as autograph. Dated

139 (plate XLI)

140

between 1490 and 1495 by Bode, Horne and Bettini; between 1497 and 1500 by other scholars. Cut on the right, where the red curtain continued. The face of the servant is much damaged, while Judith's is well preserved.

141 ⊞ ⊕ 1496 🗏 ⋮

St Francis Formerly Florence, Monastery of Sta Maria di Monticelli
From payments made in 1496 (see *Outline Biography*), it is clear that Botticelli painted this work. It was probably done in fresco and was destroyed when the building was demolished in 1529–30.

142 A

142 B

142 C

142 D

Scenes from the Life of St Zenobius

There are four panels that formed part of a backrest, probably for some Florentine confraternity, though perhaps not the Compagnia di S. Zanobi, as Rumohr thought [1827] (without citing any sources) and Poggi denied [1916]. The probable source of the subject was indicated by Horne as the *Summa historialis* of St Antoninus (Basle, 1491). Early works, according to Cavalcaselle [1864] and J. P. Richter [1910 and 1915]; late works (1498–c. 1500) for Ulmann and later scholars, with dating between c. 1495 [L. M. Richter, 1913; to Bode, 1926] and 1500–c. 1505 [Horne; to Salvini].

142 A ▦ ◔ 66,5×149,5 1495–1500 ▤ :
The Calling of St Zenobius London, National Gallery
From left to right: St Zenobius (4th-5th cent.) renounces marriage; he is baptized by Bishop Theodosius; with his father he attends his mother's baptism; he is consecrated bishop by Pope Damasus. Together with 142 B., it became known in 1891, when the two pictures went from the Rondinelli house, Florence, to the Mond Collection, London, from which it passed (1924) to the National Gallery after having been exhibited (1894) as autograph in a show at Burlington House.

142 B ▦ ◔ 65×139,5 1495–1500 ▤ :
Three Miracles of St Zenobius London, National Gallery
The setting is the square in Florence now called S. Pier Maggiore. Beyond the arch on the right is Borgo Pinti. From left to right: St Zenobius frees two youths from the curse of their mother, whom they had mistreated; raises the son of a French lady, who had been left in the saint's charge when she went on pilgrimage to Rome; restores the sight of a man who promised to become a Christian convert if cured. The panel's history is the same as 142 A.

142 C ▦ ◔ 67,3×150,5 1495–1500 ▤ :
Four Miracles of St Zenobius New York, Metropolitan Museum
From left to right: Zenobius raises a dead man; heals a man fallen from a horse;

(background, under a loggia) heals sick man; enables Deacon Eugenius to resuscitate or heal a woman. The panel went from Milan to Berlin. With the sale of the Abdy Collection, London (1911), it went to the Metropolitan (and then published by Burroughs). A relatively recent restoration removed extensive repainting, revealing, among other things, the coffin with two skeletons in the center.

142 D ▦ ◔ 66×182 1495–1500 ▤ :
The Death of St Zenobius Dresden, Gemäldegalerie
The setting is a much idealized reconstruction of the former Cathedral and Archbishop's Palace, Florence. From left to right: a child is crushed by a cart; the child is carried by Deacon Eugenius to Zenobius; Zenobius revives him and returns him to his family; Zenobious announces his own imminent death. At the beginning of the nineteenth century the picture was in the Metzger Collection, Florence, whence it passed to the Von Quandt Collection, Dresden (when it was published in *Kunstblatt* [1823–4]), and then to the gallery.

143 ▦ ◔ *1497 ▤ ⦂
Unknown subject Formerly Florence, Villa of Castello
An ornamental work, probably fresco, known from payments made in 1497 (see *Outline Biography*).

Stories of Illustrious Women

Vasari mentions that, in Florence, "in Via de' Servi, in the home [of] Giovanni Vespucci, now that of Piero Salviati," Botticelli "painted all around the room several pictures with vivid and beautiful figures framed in walnut for benchbacks and woodwork." Morelli [1890] thought that 144 A. was part of the series; Ulmann thought 144 B. was also part of it and dated them 1490–1500. Later it was learned [Horne] that the house had been purchased not by Giovanni Vespucci, but by his father, Guidantonio, in 1499; the pictures were assigned that date, with some disagreement [Bode: 1492; Van Marle: 1497–1500]. It is possible, however, that the

two subjects were painted with political intent – a condemnation of despotic government.

144 A ▦ ◔ 86×165 1500* ▤
Virginia Bergamo, Accademia Carrara
The story comes from Livy and Valerius Maximus. On the left, Marcus Claudius urges Virginia to accede to Appius Claudius' wishes; when she refuses, the young woman is taken to the tribunal, where Appius condemns her to slavery notwithstanding the speech of her fiancé and father (who has arrived from his camp). On the right, Virginia's father slays her to spare her the shame and returns to camp. In the center foreground, the tumult of the warriors ends with the slaying of Appius. Acquired by Morelli in Rome (where he exhibited it as Botticelli's in 1870) and left to the academy. It is usually considered superior to 144 B., but the latter seems superior, though Botticelli may have collaborated on *Virginia*.

144 B ▦ ◔ 80×178 1500* ▤ :
Lucretia Boston, Isabella Stewart Gardner Museum
The literary sources are the same as for 144 A. On the left, Lucretia tries to resist Sextus, the son of Tarquin the Proud (or Tarquin himself). The story of Judith is depicted on the frieze above. On the right, the suicide of the violated Lucretia. On the frieze above the arch is depicted the feat of Horatius at the bridge. In the center, Brutus shows Lucretia's body to the soldiers and incites them to revolt. In the friezes of the triumphal arch are the stories of Curtius and Mucius Scaevola. In 1893–4, when the picture was exhibited in London as Botticelli's, it belonged to the Ashburnham Collection. Shortly thereafter it went to America.

145 ▦ ◔ 53×35 1499* ▤ :
The Agony in the Garden Granada, Capilla de los Reyes
Published by Gomez Moreno [1908] among the works decorating the doors of a reliquary ordered by Isabella the Catholic for a chapel she had had built in Granada just before 1504. Bertaux [1908] attributed it to the school, but it has been accepted as autograph by almost all later scholars

[from Yashiro to Salvini], with the exception of A. Venturi and others who ignore it. The usual dating is 1500–4, though Salvini dates it slightly earlier because of stylistic similarities to 144 A and B.

146 ▦ ◔ 49,5×58,5 1500* ▤ :
The Annunciation Glasgow, Art Gallery and Museum
From the McLellan Collection, Glasgow. A composition of pure

145

and intense rhythm, considered autograph – since Waagen [1854] – by most scholars, except A. Venturi, Berenson, Mesnil and Chastel, whose doubts only regard the execution. Generally dated about 1500.

147 ▦ ◔ 130×95 ▤ :
The Flight into Egypt Paris, Musée Jacquemart-André
Evidently conceived by Botticelli, but executed by the workshop, as most scholars believe, except for Bode,

Ulmann and Schmarsow [1923], who consider it autograph. It may be a copy, by a northern European artist, of a lost original. Originally on panel.

148 ▦ ◔ 108,5×75 1501 ▤ :
The Mystic Nativity London, National Gallery
In addition to the scrolls with *Gloria in excelsis Deo* and

Pax hominibus (after the Gospel According to St Luke), there is a Greek inscription on three lines at the top: "I, Sandro, painted this picture at the end of the year 1500 [Florentine calendar, hence early 1501] during the tribulations of Italy in the half time after the time, in accordance with the eleventh chapter of St John in the second woe of the Apocalypse, during the unchaining of the devil for three and a half years; then he will be [word rubbed out but generally interpreted as "fettered" or "cast out"] in

144 A

144 B (plate LVII)

accordance with the twelfth chapter, as in this picture." The "tribulations" may refer to the French invasion, to the internal troubles of Florence after the death of Lorenzo the Magnificent, or to the campaign of Cesare Borgia, who besieged Faenza in 1501 and threatened Tuscany. As for the *Apocalypse*, the "second woe" of the eleventh chapter prophesies the oppression of the "holy city ... forty and two months" by the Gentiles. In the twelfth chapter it is foreseen that Satan will be cast out "into the earth, and his angels." The expression "in the half time after the time" echoes the phrase in the *Apocalypse* (12:14), "for a time, and times, and half a time," which Savonarola interpreted (in a gloss of the Vulgate) as "a year and two years and the half of a year." This gave rise to various opinions, among scholars, about the precise period of time that would suggest (*i.e.*, the beginning of the Borgia wars or the martyrdom

Modern drawing of painting 149, from Reinach [1906].

Charity — who appear as angels on the roof [Pope-Hennessy]. Other elements, such as the pennants with litanies and the golden crowns hanging from olive branches, recall the sacred processions that Savonarola himself organized. Likewise, there are no "modern" personages; Savonarola violently opposed their appearance in sacred paintings.

5 May, 1911, no. 86) and Von Nemes (Sale Catalogue, 17 June, 1913) consider this panel autograph. Its present whereabouts are unknown. The kneeling Madonna adoring Christ on the right, with the young St John, are common in the works of Botticelli's early maturity. The standing St Joseph and the two shepherds are similar to those in *The Mystic Nativity* (148), and the ox and ass come from the Washington *tondo* (124). The stall of trunks and the ruined wall in a mountain landscape are similar to other compositions by Botticelli. But the heterogeneity of the similarities suggests it is workshop.

150 ⊞ ✇ 73×51 1500-05· 🗐 ⦂

The Mystic Crucifixion
Cambridge, Mass., Fogg Art Museum
Published by Horne [1908], who related it to the theme of the sermon Savonarola gave on 13 January 1495: "In my

148 (plates LXII-LXIV)

146

of Savonarola). Botticelli may not have had Savonarola's gloss in mind [Salvini], nor do we know the general sense of Savonarola's comments because the forty-two sermons he dedicated to the *Apocalypse* are lost. Nevertheless there remains the remarkable iconography of the dance of the hosannahing angels in the sky and the embracing of terrestrial and heavenly beings below that is hard to disconnect from Savonarola's prophetic vision of the liberation of humanity from the tribulations into which it was plunged by the coming of the Anti-Christ, effected by the political "tribulations" and the condemnation of Savonarola [Salvini]. Furthermore the Nativity is depicted in accordance with the tone of the Christmas homilies proffered by Savonarola in 1493 and 1494, when he called on the Florentines to make Florence a new Nazareth, to assemble ideally around the manger where the Madonna adored Christ, with three maidens — Grace, Truth and Justice (or rather, given the color of their clothes: Faith, Hope and

(Salvini is right to reject the identification of the three men who embrace angels in the foreground as Savonarola and two fellows in martyrdom.) About 1800 the picture was acquired by W. Y. Ottley at the sale at Villa Aldobrandini, Rome; the picture may have come from the Florence Aldobrandinis. In 1811 it was sold for £42, and in 1837 for little more than £24. In 1851 it went to the Fuller Maitland Collection (Stansted Hall, Essex), whence it was sold (1878) to the National Gallery for £1,500.

A partial replica (in *tondo*) of the Madonna and St Joseph (with young St John) adoring Christ (in a room with a ruined wall in the foreground another to the right and one in the background; a room of boughs and branches; and a hilly landscape on the left) is in the Wickham Flower Collection, London.

149 ⊞ ✇ ——— 🗐 ⦂

The Nativity Formerly
Budapest, Von Nemes Collection
Reinach and the catalogues of the collections of Sir William Neville Abdy (Sale Catalogue,

147

imagination I saw a black cross over the Babylon of Rome, and on it was written *Ira Domini*, and above it rained ... every weapon and hailstones and stones, with thunder and lightning ... and dark and abysmal weather. And I saw another cross, a golden one, that came from the sky to earth over Jerusalem, and on it was written *Misericordia Dei*, and there the weather was serene, clear, and very bright ... And I saw angels arrive with the red cross ..." In the picture, in fact, a cross is descending from heaven; on the left is Florence illuminated by the sun and angels in the sky with the red-cross shield; God blessing in a nimbus; to the right of the Cross, in storm clouds, are devils hurling flaming torches; and at the foot of the Cross an angel whips an animal while a woman embraces the holy wood. The animal has been interpreted as the fox who spoils the vines (Song of Solomon, 2:15), *i.e.*, vice [Horne], or as pagan licentiousness [Gamba; Mesnil]. It has also been interpreted as a lion, the Florentine Marzocco, *i.e.*, Florence [Bode, 1921 and

1926; Pope-Hennessy]. The beast in flight would be the wolf of corruption [Pope-Hennessy; Salvini]. Hence the following interpretations of the whole vision: Divine Wrath falls on sinful Florence, and Mary Magdalene represents the penitence of Florence [Horne; Bode]. Divine protection preserves the walls of Florence from the flames, and with the punishment of pagan Humanism (the fox) the true faith triumphs [Gamba; Mesnil]. With the punishment of the city (the lion) and the penitence of the Church (Mary Magdalene), corruption (the fox) is put to flight [Pope-

Hennessy]. Florence and the Church are purified by the angels who drive away the storm clouds and by the punishment of the Marzocco (symbol of corrupt Florence) and the wolf (corruption of the Church) [Salvini]. Thus the penitence of Florence drives away peril. In this case the immediate inspiration might have been the withdrawal of Cesare Borgia's army from Florentine territory (1502) [Gamba and others]. The canvas was acquired in Florence about 1900 and was in the Aynard Collection, Lyons. For Horne, it is Botticelli's with much

150

collaboration. When some of the repainting was removed in 1929, much of the original was missing, making accurate judgment of authorship difficult. But most scholars believe it is largely autograph.

A partial replica – of the Crucifixion only (32 × 25·5 cm.) – painted with a certain sensitivity, went (1939) to the Samuel H. Kress Collection and thence to the National Gallery, Washington.

151 🔲 🔘 220×190 / 1500–05 📭 ⋮

The Trinity with Saints
London, Courtauld Galleries
(Lee of Fareham Collection)

153

Much discussed because of the unusual composition and the many elements uncharacteristic of Botticelli's iconography. Yashiro first attributed it to Botticelli [1925] and identified it as the Convertite Altarpiece (27). The attribution was accepted by most scholars but challenged by Mesnil and Berenson [1932] and rejected by Salvini, who, because of the heterogeneity of stylistic and iconographic elements, suggested that it was a workshop production incorporating elements from various periods of Botticelli's activity. The dating is also much debated: from 1474,

151

At the foot of the Cross are the letters S B, perhaps indicating "Sandro Botticelli." Flanking the Cross are Mary Magdalene and John the Baptist, and in the left fore-ground are Tobias and the Angel. Acquired at the Monte di Pietà (i.e. pawnshop), Rome, by Sir Henry Layard; then in the Winborne Collection and then at White Lodge, Richmond Park. London.

Yashiro's dating, to 1490–5 [Bode] and many intermediate datings. Bascially it recalls, albeit in larger format, the Pallavicini *Transfiguration* (131), and incorporates a large number of disparate elements. In composition it is similar to the *Crucifixions* of Andrea del Castagno [Bettini] and the *Trinity* of Pesellino and Filippino Lippi in the National Gallery. More Botticellian are

the figures of Tobias and the Angel. Thus one might imagine - according to Salvini - that on the death of Botticelli, his followers removed some of the less attractive parts of an allegorical composition, such as *The Mystic Nativity* or *The Mystic Crucifixion,* and, for an undemanding client, sub-stituted other elements in haste, thereby giving the impression of a painting executed in successive stages. Or it might be a painting that Botticelli began and never finished, without leaving a general plan of composition, that was completed by the workshop. The edges seem mutilated and there may have been a lunette above the picture that gave it a more harmonious effect despite the weaknesses of composition.

Similar to the more Botticellian elements in this picture is the *predella* described below (152).

Scenes from the Life of Mary Magdalene

There are four panels that were sold in Florence (c 1910) and went to the Philadelphia Museum of Art with the Johnson Collection. Attributed to Botticelli by Berenson [1913] and Horne [1913], who considered it the *predella* of the Convertite Altarpiece and thus dated it shortly after 1470. Yashiro, who considered it the *predella* of the Lee of Fareham *Trinity* (151), dated

it about 1474, A. Venturi [1925] accepted Horne's attribution but dated it 1481, while Bode [1926] dated it 1490–5 because of its "Savonarolian" intensity. Van Marle and L. Venturi [1931] accepted the attribution, but the latter dated it 1481–90. Gamba – who considered the Convertite panel to be the one in the Uffizi (27) – dated this *predella* about 1471, and his dating was accepted by Mesnil, Bettini and Salvini. Although Salvini rightly pointed out the timbre of Pollaiuolo in the drawing, the *predella* still seems a late work. In this respect, compare the figure of Mary Magdalene in 152 D with that in the London *Trinity* (151) or that of the observer of the Ascension in the same panel with certain figures in *The Mystic Nativity* (148). The symbols shown below apply to all four sections of the *predella*.

152 🔲 🔘 18×42 / 1500* 📭 ⋮

A The Magdalene listens to Christ preaching

B The Magdalene bathes Christ's Feet

C Noli Me Tangere

D The Magdalene's Communion and Ascension
These two events actually concern the life of St Mary of Egypt, but by the fifteenth century this confusion was common.

154 A

154 B

154 C

153 🔲 🔘 107,5×173 📭 ⋮

Incomplete Adoration of the Magi Florence, Soprintendenza alle Gallerie
Heat Wilson [1880] suggested that in the figure to the left of St Joseph was depicted Savonarola, who embraces Lorenzo the Magnificent and points to Jesus. Heat Wilson also thought that there were portraits of Benivieni and Leonardo in this picture, but these identifications seem very unlikely. The picture went to its present location in 1779 and was on exhibit from 1880 to 1940 as work done in chiaroscuro by Botticelli and colored in the seventeenth century. The attribution was confirmed by Heat, who considered it a late work, followed by Ulmann and

152 A

152 C

152 B

152 D

Ridolfi [1896], while F. O. Schulze [1880] assigned it to a follower. Ulmann thought the picture might be one mentioned by the Anonimo Gaddiano in Palazzo Vecchio, "above the staircase that goes to the Catena"; but Horne rejected this hypothesis, since that picture would have been frescoed. Müller-Walde [1889] and Müntz [1897] were the first to recognize elements of Leonardo in the picture. Ridolfi thought this was due to the influence of Leonardo's unfinished *Epiphany* in the Uffizi, and his hypothesis was confirmed by Bettini. Horne dated the work before 1480, while Yashiro dated it a couple of years later. Other scholars date it much later, just before [A. Venturi; Van Marle; Gamba; Mesnil; Salvini] or just after [Bode; Schmarsow; Bettini] the year 1500.

Fragmentary Adoration of the Magi

Originally this picture must have been very similar to 153 and, like that one, only drawn in chiaroscuro. The three surviving pieces were together until 1884 in the W. Russell Collection, London, first attributed to Filippino Lippi and then to Botticelli (see also 154 C). The attribution to Botticelli was rejected by Horne [1903, 1908, 1909–10], who considered the pieces parts of an old copy of a lost original, perhaps frescoed in Palazzo Vecchio, Florence (see 153). But the attribution was resumed by Yashiro [1929] and most later scholars [until Salvini] accepted it. Most date it about 1490, but Salvini and the present writer believe it to be contemporary with 153.

154 A ▦ ⊗ 17,5×19 1500-05 ▤⦂

Onlookers and Horses New York, Pierpont Morgan Library
Referring to 153, this fragment must have been on the left in the original. From the Russel Collection it went to the Salting, where Ulmann attributed it to Botticelli. Then it went to the Fairfax Murray Collection.

154 B ▦ ⊗ 30×25 1500-05 ▤⦂

Holy Family with one of the Magi Cambridge, Fitzwilliam Museum
This must have been the central part of the original. At the sale of the Russel Collection it went to the Brough of Leck (Stafford) Collection and later went to Cambridge.

154 C ▦ ⊗ 44×37 1500-05 ▤⦂

Onlookers Cambridge, Fitzwilliam Museum
This comprises two pieces, the larger of which was published by W. Young Ottley in 1823 as the work of Filippino Lippi.

This piece went from the Russel to the Knowles Collection and then to the Clough Collection, London. The smaller piece, lost from

Works formerly attributed to Botticelli

Below are listed paintings that, despite authoritative attribution to Botticelli, seem so alien to his corpus that they cannot be inserted in the chronological catalogue of his works. They are listed in alphabetical order under the name of city in which they are located (except for 174).

155. Portrait of a Young Man Berlin, Staatliche Museen
Panel (41 × 31 cm.). In Berlin since 1829 and considered a work by Filippino Lippi until Morelli correctly identified the author as Raffaellino del Garbo, an attribution accepted by many scholars [Berenson; Bodmer, 1931; to Berti and Baldini, 1957; Salvini]. Ulmann assigned it to a disciple of Sandro or Filippino under the influence of Perugino; Bode attributed it to Botticelli, while others [e.g., Scharf, 1935] referred it to Lippi.

156. Portrait of a Young Woman Berlin, Staatliche Museen
Panel (47·5 × 35 cm.)

155

156

Published by Bode [1888] as as autograph and probably a portrait of Simonetta Vespucci, first dating it [1921] about 1480, and later [1926] about 1476. Schmarsow and Van Marle also considered it autograph, the former dating it about 1480–1, and the latter considering the subject to be Lucrezia Tornabuoni. Ulmann

sight after the Russel sale, reappeared in 1896 at a Sotheby sale and was acquired by Clough, who later bought the larger piece.

considered it workshop [1893] as did Berenson, Gamba (who identified the subject as Clarice Orsini and dated it about 1485), L. Venturi, Mesnil and Salvini, though Salvini found the work inferior to other workshop paintings. Thus it is possible that the picture is the work of a very late imitator.

157. Portrait of a Youth Besançon, Musée des Beaux-

157
Arts (Gigoux Bequest)
Panel (46 × 31 cm.). It bears the legend *El tempo consuma*. Formerly ascribed to Masaccio, Verrocchio or Botticini [A. Venturi, 1911], Piero Pollaiuolo [Berenson, 1936] or school [Van Marle, 1929], a non-Florentine painter [Sabatini, 1944], Antonio Pollaiuolo [Ragghianti, 1949] or a weak follower [Ortolani, 1949], Cossa [Meiss, 1951], etc. At one time Berenson [1932] and Mesnil considered it Botticelli's. But it seems to be neither his nor his workshop's [Salvini], but it might be by Mariano d'Antonio.

158. The Redeemer with the Crown of Thorns Birmingham, Alabama, Museum of Art
Panel. Formerly New York, the property of Kleinberger, who published it as autograph, followed by Van Marle [1931]. Berenson, in his last catalogues, attributes it to Jacopo del Sellaio.

**159. The Adoration of the Magi with Saints Catherine

The Triumph of Religion, *one of the four* Allegories *in Fiesole.*

159
and Andrew** Dijon, Musée des États de Bourgogne (J. Maciet Bequest). Panel (33 × 39 cm.). In the museum since 1897. For Berenson, a copy of lost original by Botticelli. Many scholars, including Geiger [1966 museum catalogue], ascribe it to Jacopo del Sellaio. It seems rather closer to Pesellino.

160. Allegories Fiesole, Museo Bandini
A series of four panels – the

158

triumphs of Chastity, Love, Time and Religion – from the Oratory of Sant'Ansano, Fiesole. Gebhardt [1908] considered them autograph, but more likely they are by Jacopo del Sellaio.

161. The Death of Lucretia Florence, Pitti
Panel (42 × 126 cm.). Iconographically linked to the similar subject in Boston (144 B) and now generally attributed to Filippino Lippi as a painting derived from the Boston one. Berenson (at least at first) and Yashiro considered it Botticelli's workshop, and Mesnil ascribed it to Botticelli.

162. The Crucifixion Frankfurt, Städelsches Kunstinstitut
Panel *tondo*. According to Berenson [1953], it is a copy of a lost original. Probably a posthumous imitator.

163. Portrait of a Young Man Formerly Heemstede (Haarlem), Gutman Collection
It went to its last known

161

owner about 1930 from the Von Nemes Collection, Budapest. Autograph for Uhde-Bernays [1913], A. Venturi [1925] and Van

and attributed to Andrea del Castagno. Fry [1930] attributed both to Botticelli, while other scholars ascribe them to Bartolomeo di

published and condemned for heresy. According to Palmieri, every human being incarnates one of the angels who, at the time of Lucifer's rebellion, remained neutral. Palmieri intended the painting for his family chapel in S. Pier Maggiore, Florence. The panel, covered because it included the portrait of its heretical owner, was in that church until 1785. It then went to the Palmieri house and (after 1808) it went to the Hamilton Collection and finally (1882) to the National Gallery. Vasari's attribution was accepted by Mesnil and Brizio [1933], while Bode [1886] related it to a group of pictures that turned out to be Botticini's, to whom the work is now generally ascribed.

166. Portrait of a Man
London, National Gallery
Panel (51·5 × 35 cm.) It passed from the Arrigoni Collection, Bergamo, to the Layard, Venice (1865), and finally to the museum (1916), where — abandoning former attributions to Dürer, Foppa and Signorelli — it was catalogued

165

170

162

163

166

167

173

as a Botticelli. Berenson [1932] and Vertova [1952] agreed. Holmes [1918], Van Marle, Scharf [1933], Neilson [1938], Davies [1951] and Salvini attribute it to Raffaellino del Garbo.

167. St Barbara Lucca, Pinacoteca

Esther (?) leaving the Palace of Ahasuerus *(see 174).*
(Below) Presentation of the Virgins to Ahasuerus *(see 174).*

Panel. Traditionally considered autograph, but later ascribed to the workshop. Modern criticism tends to ascribe it to Botticini.

168. Madonna and Child with Young St John Formerly Munich, Von Nemes Collection
Panel (89 × 68 cm.). It passed from the collection of Cardinal Fesch (1837) to the Spiridon Collection, Paris, and then (1929) to Von Nemes. Ascribed to Botticelli by Fischel [1929] but rejected by other scholars.

169. Madonna and Child
New York, Blumenthal Collection
Panel (fragmentary; 45 × 32 cm.) Formerly in the Butler Collection, London, and then in the Hainauer, Berlin. Attributed to Botticelli by Berenson [1932 etc.].

170. The Seasons New York, Knoedler Property

172

A series of four panels depicting Spring (78 × 21 cm.), Summer (78 × 21), Autumn (76 × 215) and Winter (80 × 23).
Formerly in the Hannah de Rothschild Collection, where in 1878 they were catalogued as autograph; later in the Rosenberg Collection, London. A. Venturi still [1937]

Marle; rejected by Berenson [1932] and Salvini. Probably the work of Mariano d'Antonio whose self-portrait it might be.

164. A Scene from the Life of St Andrew Liverpool, Walker Art Gallery
Panel (25 × 50 cm.).
Formerly in the Roscoe Collection together with a *Martyrdom of St Sebastian*, both of which probably belonged to the same *predella*,

Giovanni in the period after he had left Botticelli's workshop.

165. The Assumption of the Virgin London, National Gallery
Canvas (transferred from panel; 225 × 458 cm.).
Vasari states that this picture was commissioned from Botticelli by Matteo Palmieri (d 1478) and that the subject came from Palmieri's book *Città di vita*, posthumously

considered them autograph, although Ulmann had already [1893] expressed serious doubts about the execution, doubts shared by most scholars.

171. Scenes from the Life of Virginia Paris, Louvre Panel (41 × 125 cm.). Iconographically very close to the painting of the same subject in Bergamo (144 A). It is now generally ascribed to Filippino Lippi and considered a pendant of 161. Berenson at first and Yashiro attributed it to Botticelli, while Mesnil considered it a workshop painting in which Botticelli might have had more of a hand than in the Bergamo painting.

172. The Holy Family Pistoia, Museo Civico
Canvas (63 × 48 cm.). From the Rospigliosi Collection, Rome. Traditionally considered Botticelli. Berenson considered it workshop. Melani [1966 Museum Catalogue], pointed out among other things, that it is executed in oils, rejects it as the work of any member of Botticelli's circle and ascribes it to a posthumous imitator. A copy (canvas, 62 × 47 cm.) in the Städelsches Kunstinstitut, Frankfurt, seems to have been executed by the same painter who did the *Christ* that was formerly in the Lazzaroni Collection (136). Another copy (panel, 32 × 21 cm.) in the Museen der Künste, Leipzig, albeit considered the

prototype of all these pictures by Mesnil, is also probably the work of an imitator outside Botticelli's workshop.

173. The Vestal Virgins Rouen, Musée des Beaux-Arts Panel. Related to *Virginia* and *Lucretia* (144 A and B). The museum considers it autograph, but it was probably painted by a member of Filippino Lippi's circle.

174. Scenes from the Life of Esther
There are two series of panels that once were part of two *cassoni*. After being attributed to various artists, they were considered by Wind [1950] and Chastel [1957] a collaboration between Botticelli and Filippino Lippi, together with *Derelicta*, Rome (139). All other scholars reject Botticelli's collaboration. The first of the two series would have included – in additon to *Derelicta* – the following works: *The Presentation of the Virgins to Ahasuerus* (47 × 138 cm.; Chantilly, Musée Condé) and *The Revocation of the Edicts against the Jews* (47 × 138 cm.; Paris, De Vogüé Collection). The second would have included: *Mordecai honoured by Haman* (48 × 42 cm.; Vaduz, Liechtenstein Collection), *Esther before the Palace of Ahasuerus* (48 × 138 cm.; Vaduz, Liechtenstein Collection), and *Esther (or Vashti) leaving the Palace of Ahasuerus* (46 × 40 cm.; Florence, Fondazione Horne).

Other works mentioned in sources

Listed below are works mentioned in the sources – Anonimo Gaddiano, Vasari, archive documents, etc. – which, although possibly attributable to Botticelli, are not included in the Catalogue because of the lack of chronological information.

Florence
Trofei House
175. A panel showing the Madonna and Child with an angel and young St John, mentioned by Borghini [1584]. It might be a work already in the Catalogue, but it is impossible to identify it with certainty.
Church of Orsanmichele
176. Vasari mentioned a baldachin "full of Our Ladies all different and beautiful" painted in a technique that rendered the painting indelible and made the figures visible from both sides of the cloth.
Church of S. Pier Gattolini
177. The Anonimo Gaddiano mentioned a panel on the main altar without mentioning the subject. It is not known what happened to the picture after the church was demolished under Cosimo I to make way for new fortifications.
The Cathedral
178. Cartoons for mosaics for the vault of the Chapel of S. Zanobi. They were begun in 1491 but never finished.

The Guardaroba Mediceo
179. Vasari mentions a "Bacchus raising a bowl to his lips." What was certainly there at the same time, according to to the inventory, was "a portrait of Bacchus, on canvas, three *braccia* high".
Palazzo Medici
180. A bed headboard in the antechamber of Piero de' Medici, with a "Fortune from the hand of Sandro di Botticello," inventoried at the death of Lorenzo the Magnificent (1492).
181. Vasari mentions "two heads of women in profile, very beautiful."
Palazzo della Signoria (Palazzo Vecchio)
182. Anonimo Gaddiano mentions an *Adoration of the Magi* painted – probably in fresco – at the head of the stairs before the Porta della Catena, in the inner courtyard. It disappeared during refurbishing under Vasari's direction. Attempts have been made to identify it (see 153 and 154), but unsuccessfully.
183. The inventory of Palazzo Vecchio for 1647 mentions a painting depicting a nude Galatea with other figures.

Montevarchi
Church of S. Francesco
184. Vasari mentions that a panel on the main altar was painted by Botticelli but does not describe the subject.

Botticelli's other artistic activities

In addition to the few drawings in the Catalogue (63 C, 70 and 132), others are reproduced below. Together with some others (whose attribution is controversial) and the illustrations of Dante's Divine Comedy *(pp. 114–15), these comprise the surviving corpus of Botticelli's drawings.*

(Above) Head of a Young Man (diam. 75 mm.; London, British Museum), perhaps a sketch for angels in paintings similar to 15, 18 etc. Angel in Flight (92 × 95 mm.; Bologna, private collection), published by Bertini [1953], who dated it c. 1490. (Right) Pallas (190 × 66 mm.; Milan, Biblioteca Ambrosiana), formerly ascribed to Filippino Lippi; attributed to Botticelli by Berenson and dated after 1490.

(Above) Angel (270 × 180 mm.; Florence, Gabinetto degli Uffizi); the traditional attribution to Botticelli is almost unanimously accepted; dating varies between 1483 and c. 1490, the latter favored by modern critics. Pallas (220 × 240 mm.; same location), traditionally ascribed to Botticelli (but workshop for Horne and Berenson). For Horne and others, a sketch for a tapestry of Guy de Beaudreuil (still owned by the commissioner's descendants, Fevelles), woven after 1491, which date is also assigned to the sketch. (Below) St Thomas (175 × 120 mm.; Milan, Biblioteca Ambrosiana), considered preparatory for the engraving of The Assumption (see p. 117); traditional attribution generally accepted. The Nativity (160 × 260 mm.; Florence, Gabinetto degli Uffizi), generally accepted as Botticelli (for Morelli [1891–2 etc.], school) and dated to c. 1495 despite similarities to The Mystic Nativity *(148).*

Vasari writes that on Botticelli's return from Rome after his work in the Sistine Chapel (1482) he illustrated Dante's *Inferno*. This refers to the drawings, probably engraved by Baccio Baldini, that illustrated the edition of Dante edited by Landino and published as early as 1481. This means that Botticelli did not do them after his return from Rome. Nevertheless Vasari is probably right in saying that Botticelli spent a great deal of time on these illustrations. The Anonimo Gaddiano mentions that Botticelli "painted and depicted Dante on parchment for Lorenzo di Pierfrancesco de' Medici, which was a marvelous thing." Most of these parchments were acquired in Paris (1803) from the bookseller Molini by the Duke of Hamilton, in whose collection (Glasgow) Waagen [1854] saw them. He ascribed them to Botticelli and others. The parchments went (1882) to the Kupferstichkabinett, Berlin (but they were divided between East and West Berlin after World War II), and were studied at once by Lippmann, Rosenberg and Epherussi, all of whom agreed in the total attribution to Botticelli, as have subsequent scholars. In 1886 other sheets were discovered in a miscellany (formerly Queen Christina of Sweden's) in the Vatican Library [Strzygowski, 1887; Pér/até, 1887]. The sheets in dimension from 32·7–34 × 47–47·4 cm. On the back of each is the text of a Canto, in a fine hand, referring to the drawing on the succeeding page. The drawings are in silverpoint and lead (with much overlay in pen and some damage to the drawings, which are still generally visible and on some sheets incomplete). The surviving drawings are: the plan of *Inferno* (recto) and the illustration for Canto I and those for Cantos IX–XVI, Vatican; those for Cantos VIII and XVII–XXXIV (two sheets for this last) of *Inferno*, all 33 of *Purgatorio* (and the plan), and 31 of *Paradiso* (except XXX and XXXIII, blank pages), Berlin. According to Horne, they were drawn between 1490 and 1496, the year Lorenzo di Pierfrancesco fled.

(Above) Inferno, Canto XIII (Vatican), detail. At Virgil's request, Dante breaks a branch that contains the soul of Pier delle Vigne; below Dante, a harpy; the two crouching nudes attacked by dogs refer to Lano del Toppo and Giacomo da Santandrea; before the lower nude, Dante reassembles branches with the soul of Lotto degli Agli (or Rocco de' Mozzi).

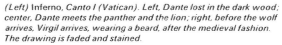

(Left) Inferno, Canto I (Vatican). Left, Dante lost in the dark wood; center, Dante meets the panther and the lion; right, before the wolf arrives, Virgil arrives, wearing a beard, after the medieval fashion. The drawing is faded and stained.

(Above) Inferno, Canto VIII (Vatican). To the sides above, the people in the mud and Phlegyas' boat in the swamp of Dis; below, left, Dante and Virgil (shown four times) approach the city of Dis, on whose tower are the Erinnyes, while the devils, admonished by the divine messenger, appear at the gate; right, the two poets among the flaming tombs of the heresiarchs. (Right) Inferno, Canto XXVI (Berlin). Above, left, the poets emerge from the rock and stop on the stone bridge to look at the flames of the counselors of fraud in the eighth bowge (the forked flame alludes to Ulysses and Diomedes).

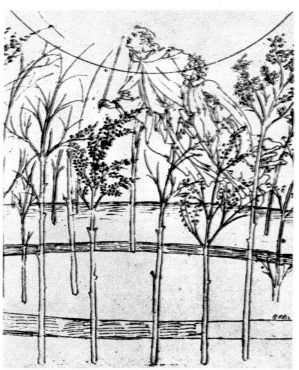

(Above), Inferno, Canto XXXI (Berlin), detail. The two poets (left and center) and the chained giants (including Nimrod with the horn and Antaeus leaning over Virgil and Dante). (Below), Purgatorio, Canto III (Berlin). The angel boatman goes back (above, center); the souls that have just disembarked (left) run to the mountain, as do Virgil and Dante (left and center); Dante shows Virgil a group of souls (right) who block their way. Perhaps unfinished. (Right) Paradiso, Canto I (Berlin), detail. Beatrice and Dante take flight from the earthly paradise towards the first mobile.

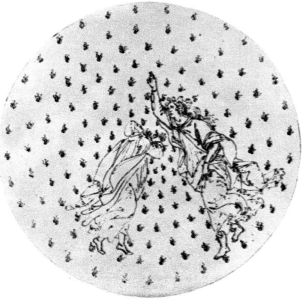

(Below) Purgatorio, Canto XI (Berlin). Dante and Virgil (shown three times) pass through the circle of the proud: center, the story of Aldobrandeschi; left, that of Oderisi da Gubbio. Perhaps unfinished. (Right, above) Paradiso, Canto VI (Berlin). Dante and Beatrice in the heaven of Mercury with the "lights" of active spirits. (Right, below) Paradiso, Canto XXI (Berlin). Beatrice and Dante (shown twice) in the heaven of Saturn, at the foot and on the celestial ladder with blessed souls flying (depicted as little angels).

No contemporary document or historian mentions
Botticelli as a designer of inlay. Vasari does say that there
was a great revival of this art in Florence at the time of
Brunelleschi and Paolo Uccello, although it probably
began somewhat later, about 1450. Within that revival,
modern scholars – thanks chiefly to Longhi [*Piero della
Francesca*, 1927] and Arcangeli [*Tarsie*, 1943] – have also
set Botticelli alongside Piero and Baldovinetti. They have
attributed to Botticelli the plans for the door of the Sala dei
Gigli, Palazzo Vecchio, Florence, and various undertakings
in the Palazzo Ducale, Urbino. At one time the Florence
project was attributed to Domenico Ghirlandaio, but all
now ascribe it to Botticelli. The preparatory sketches for
Urbino were once ascribed to Piero della Francesca and
Botticelli jointly [E. Calzini, 1899], then to Baccio Pontelli
[Budinich, 1904] or Francesco di Giorgio [L. Venturi, 1914].
Longhi attributed the work to Botticelli alone [1927], and
this has generally been accepted.

*(Below, left and center) Door panels depicting Dante and
Petrarch (Florence, Palazzo Vecchio, Sala dei Gigli), inlaid
by Francesco di Giovanni, known as Francione, and
Giuliano da Maiano, probably in 1478, when both worked
there.*

*(Above) Lower part of door, Sala degli Angeli, Palazzo
Ducale, Urbino (perhaps inlaid by Baccio Pontelli, by 1476)
showing perspectives whose conception was ascribed to
Botticelli [Salmi, 1945]. (Right) Upper part depicting
Apollo and Pallas.*

Inlay figures in the studiolo of Federico da Montefeltro, Palazzo Ducale, Urbino: Faith, Charity, Portrait of Duke Guidobaldo da Montefeltro. The execution is attributed to Baccio Pontelli; the year 1476 is inscribed on the ceiling. The inlays are in "perfect" accord with Botticelli's style at the time [Arcangeli]; there is a clear relation between Charity and the Venus in Primavera (58); the inspiration of the inlay seems more "achieved and vibrant" than that of Venus in the painting [Arcangeli].

Vasari's biography contains references to Botticelli's work in "minor" arts or, at least, to contributions he made. In particular, Vasari says that Botticelli was "one of the first to work standards and other draperies, as they say, of mosaic [*i.e.,* a sort of inlay of colored fabrics], so that they do not fade and show color on both sides of the cloth." The works that Vasari mentions have been lost (see *Catalogue* 176), but evidence survives of drawings for embroidery. (In addition to the cope cover illustrated, Botticelli is usually credited with the idea for a chasuble in S. Martino, Pietrasanta, another in Orvieto Cathedral, a tunicle in the same cathedral, a dalmatic in the Schloss Museum, Berlin, and a tapestry in the Beaudreuil Collection, Favelle [p. 113].) Vasari also mentions the woodcuts Botticelli did for Landino's edition of Dante (1481) and many other things engraved by him or, more likely, some specialist, which were "in bad fashion because the intaglio was badly done." In addition to *The Assumption* here (see also p. 113) several prints in the Gabinetto degli Uffizi, Florence, and in the British Museum have been related to Botticelli. Botticelli's influence may also be evident in such bronze plaques as the *Galatea on a Dolphin,* Fondazione Horne, Florence; *Enthroned Madonna and Child,* Bargello, Florence; and a brass sundial with the personification of Geometry, Fondazione Horne.

(Right) Another inlay in the studiolo of Federico da Montefeltro. It imitates a bookcase with a half-open grill door. It is believed that Botticelli did a preliminary drawing for this exquisitely "metaphysical" inlay, which was executed with great compositional mastery and a very subtle handling of wood tones.

(Above) Embroidered cope cover (47 × 47 cm.), with the Coronation of the Virgin, four angels and two worshipers (Milan, Museo Poldi Pezzoli). Reached the museum before 1900, design already attributed to Botticelli. Later because of the insignia shown, Santambrogio [1903] thought it had to do with Cardinal Jacopo di Lusitania and dated it 1459, too early for Botticelli. Modern scholars attribute the design to Botticelli. (Left). The Assumption of the Virgin (engraving, 825 × 260 cm.; Florence, Uffizi). Attribution to Botticelli partly confirmed by drawing of St Thomas (see p. 113).

117

Indexes

Index of subjects

The identification of some of the people in these indexes is doubtful (see the various entries in the Catalogue).

Index of titles

An asterisk after a number indicates that copies of the work are also mentioned in the Catalogue entry.

Topographical Index

An asterisk before the number indicates a replica or copy that is mentioned in the Catalogue entry for the number.

2284-20-14
22-55
10/79

Photographic sources

Color plates: De Antonis, Rome; Isabella Stewart Gardner Museum, Boston, Mass.; Mandel, Milan; National Gallery of Art, Washington D.C.; Scala, Florence; Walter Steinkopf, Berlin; Witty, Sunbury-on-Thames.
Black and white illustrations: Alinari, Florence; Art Institute, Chicago, Ill.; Mr and Mrs Martin A. Ryerson Collection, Chicago, Ill.; Baltimore Museum of Art, Mary Frick Jacobs Collection, Baltimore, Ma.; Cav. Bandieri, Modena; Fogg Museum of Art, Cambridge, Mass.; National Gallery of Art, Samuel H. Kress Collection, Washington D.C.; North Carolina Museum of Art, Samuel H. Kress Collection, Raleigh Ca.; Photographie Giraudon, Paris; Pierpont Morgan Library, New York; Rizzoli Archives, Milan; Soprintendenza alle Galerie, Florence; Staedelsches Kunstinstitut, Frankfurt.